ISBN 978-1-333-79038-7
PIBN 10548319

¶ *Of this Special Edition of THE FACE OF CHINA One Hundred and Ten Copies have been printed, of which* One *Hundred only are for Sale.*

This is No. 17

THE FACE OF CHINA

TRAVELS IN EAST, NORTH, CENTRAL AND WESTERN CHINA ¶ WITH SOME ACCOUNT OF THE NEW SCHOOLS, UNIVERSITIES, MISSIONS, AND THE OLD RELIGIOUS SACRED PLACES OF CONFUCIANISM, BUDDHISM, AND TAOISM THE WHOLE WRITTEN & ILLUSTRATED

BY E. G. KEMP, F.R.S.G.S.

LONDON
CHATTO & WINDUS
MCM IX

PORTRAIT OF AUTHOR
AS CHINESE "FEMALE TRAVELLING SCHOLAR"

THE FACE OF CHINA

TRAVELS IN EAST, NORTH, CENTRAL AND WESTERN CHINA ¶ WITH SOME ACCOUNT OF THE NEW SCHOOLS, UNIVERSITIES, MISSIONS, AND THE OLD RELIGIOUS SACRED PLACES OF CONFUCIANISM, BUDDHISM, AND TAOISM

THE WHOLE WRITTEN & ILLUSTRATED BY E. G. KEMP, F.R.S.G.S.

C W

LONDON
CHATTO & WINDUS
M CM IX

THIS BOOK

IS DEDICATED TO THE FRIEND

TO WHOSE SUGGESTION AND ENCOURAGEMENT

IT OWES ITS EXISTENCE

PRINCIPAL MARCUS DODS, D.D.

PREFACE

EVERY intelligent person that I have met whose good fairy has led him to the Celestial Empire has fallen under the spell of that marvellous people and marvellous land. I am fired with the ambition to cast that spell even on those who have never been there, by showing them as accurately and vividly as I can, with pen and brush, what the face of China actually is.

People *may* describe with success the soul of a people, provided it is sufficiently near the surface, but the foreigner who has known and loved China for a lifetime would be the first to repudiate the possibility of doing this in the case of China. I would rather take Browning's view—"Nor soul helps body more than body soul"—and try to set down faithfully the things I have seen, that they may lead others to study China for themselves.

It may be objected that the picture is too much *couleur de rose*, because I have not dwelt on the dark side of things: but there is a use for eyelids as well as for eyes.

This book is the result of a year spent in Shansi, 1893–94, and six months spent in travel through the provinces of Shantung, Chili, Hupeh, Szechwan, and Yünnan during 1907–8. The former visit was mainly spent at a medical mission at Taiyüanfu, which was then remote from Western influences; now everything has changed, and I travelled from north-east to south-west of the Empire and found no village untouched by the great awakening. On the first occasion I was always conscious of a certain hostility in the attitude of the people towards foreigners; this time it was quite the reverse. Considering the behaviour of many travellers towards the Chinese, this seems to me really astonishing; but they are very sensitive in their appreciation of mental attitude, and they responded unhesitatingly to the call we made on their chivalry by placing ourselves unreservedly in their hands. We were repeatedly warned not to do this, but our confidence was justified by the event. In no European country could we have been more courteously treated, and in very few have I travelled so happily and so free from care.

The journey was one long series of pleasant surprises, and my friend expressed the feelings of both of us when, on crossing the frontier into Burma, she exclaimed: "If only we could turn round and go all the way back again!" If any one is induced by reading this book to make personal acquaintance with China, it will not have been written in vain.

NOTE

There is so little in this volume which is drawn from other sources than personal observation, and information obtained from our Chinese and missionary friends on the spot, that I have thought well not to burden the reader with foot-notes. The various details as to the religions of China are mainly drawn from an interesting little volume by Giles, "Religions of Ancient China," Smith's "Uplift of China," and Hackmann's "Buddhism as a Religion"; while the account of the railways is from Kent's "Railway Enterprise in China."

The spelling of Chinese names is according to the most recent standard map, giving the orthography of the Chinese Imperial Post Office.

CONTENTS

ILLUSTRATIONS

Coloured Plates

Illustrations

Sepia Drawings

THE FACE OF CHINA

CHAPTER I

Shanghai

MY first voyage to China was unspeakably distasteful, and as we neared Hong Kong we were suddenly caught up in the tail of a typhoon and carried for forty-eight hours wherever it pleased to take us. Most of that time we were without food, and could not even get a cup of tea; while we found it hard work to cling to a seat. When we emerged from the storm, and steamed into the wonderful bay of Hong Kong, it seemed like Paradise; it looked to my eyes the most beautiful harbour I had ever seen: and I have seen nearly all the most celebrated ones, without feeling tempted to change my opinion. The first introduction to a new country, if it happens to be when the faculties are specially quickened, makes an indelible impression, and from this time China has been to me a land of infinite charm and beauty. The more I have seen of it, the more I have realised its fascination; even its ugliness is interesting.

Hong Kong lies along the shore, with a steep cliff rising abruptly behind it, called the Peak, and the typhoon had laid parts of it in ruins, and unroofed many of the houses, so that it was by no means looking its best. British pride swelled within me as I thought of the transformation that had taken place in half a century. When it was ceded to the British it was a barren island, with a population of 5000 inhabitants; now it is the second largest port in the Empire, with a population of 238,724. There is an immense boat population; whole families have lived from generation to generation in their boats along the shore. In Hong Kong, East and West live happily together, learning to appreciate one another. Chinese merchants are members of its council and take an active part in its government. It has become not only the greatest shipping but also the greatest banking centre of the East, and it is a significant fact that it contributes annually £20,000 to the British Treasury as its military contribution.

From Hong Kong to Shanghai is but a step, and at first sight the latter seems almost as European as the former. The landing, after coming up one of the mouths of the Yangtze River, is in the centre of a promenade, with broad grass borders between it and the road, along which lie the finest commercial buildings of the city for the distance of more than a mile. This is the Bund, the most imposing part of the concession. It may be well to mention what a "concession" is, as this is a term continually used with regard to the treaty ports, such as Tientsin, Hankow, and Shanghai. It is a right granted to Europeans to inhabit a certain defined area, to possess property in it (no private individual except a Chinaman has the right to buy land for building on, in China, although it is occasionally done in the interior), to live under European law, to have their own police and manage their own affairs. The Shanghai concession was mapped out in 1843 by Sir George (then Captain) Balfour, and is on a broad cosmopolitan basis: later on the French obtained one adjoining it, and then the Americans. Many Europeans live outside the concession, especially in a quarter where the English have laid out a charming shady road, perhaps the most tortuous in existence—so as to avoid desecrating graves; it is called the Bubbling Well Road. The concessions have their own post-offices, where you call for letters, if you happen to expect any from the country to which they belong. We found the Russian post-office up a staircase in a thoroughly unofficial-looking house.

The traveller, however, on landing at Shanghai ought not to drive along the Bund to the pleasant Astor House Hotel, but should make a détour into the Chinese streets Nankin Loo, or Foochow Loo, densely thronged streets, where nineteen out of every twenty people wear blue robes, varying in shade from deepest ultramarine to palest aquamarine. One is accustomed to think of the Chinese as quiet, slow-going people, but the traffic of Shanghai is so great that I know no place where you are more conscious of business bustle. The crowd in the streets is almost entirely composed of men and boys, so that it is hard to imagine where room is found for the women and children, even the balconies and shops as well as streets being packed with men. It is estimated that Shanghai has 160,000 inhabitants to the square mile. It is necessary to visit old Shanghai really to see what it *can* be, and it is a mistake to be deterred from doing this (as many visitors are) on account of its special squalor and dirt, or by the absurd statement that all Chinese cities are alike.

You pass into the real Shanghai through two low gateways, set at right angles from one another, where no vehicle is ever allowed to enter; indeed, such a thing is practically impossible. The streets are so narrow and tortuous that it is hard even for carriers to force a passage through the crowd. The houses are fairly high, and innumerable signboards (long, narrow boards covered with gilt characters which read from bottom to top) hanging overhead block out the light and hinder any current of air from driving away evil smells. The entrances to the shops are lined with Chinese lanterns of every shape, size, and colour: when lit, they cast a kindly glamour over the celestials below, very different from the pitiless glare of electric light. There is no gaudy display of goods in shop windows, for there are no windows; just an open counter on which a few specimens may be lying, probably in a glass case. The walls are lined from floor to ceiling with shallow drawers, filled with endless little parcels containing the rest of the stock-in-trade. Despite the squalid surroundings and the tininess of the shops, this may be very valuable (for the Chinese are great lovers of curios), jade, bronze, ivory, china, or silver. Along with such things are mixed the most absurd rubbish, mainly European goods. Many shops contain a row of finely carved chairs to accommodate purchasers, and elaborately decorated woodwork, such as screens with beautiful groups of figures at one end. We should have liked to buy many things, but this is not to be done lightly, and several days of diplomatic dealing are required before purchaser and seller can come to terms in the orthodox way. No Eastern would be satisfied with the monotony of our Western methods. The whole street is interested in the performance, and looks on as at a play. The amount of business transacted appears to be in inverse proportion to the number of shops.

We threaded our way through a maze of lanes till we came to the centre of the town—the original of the celebrated willow pattern[1]—and as picturesque a

[1] The legend of the Willow Pattern (introduced into England by Minton in 1780) is as follows:—Koong-Shee, the daughter of a wealthy mandarin, fell in love with her father's secretary, Chang. She had been already affianced to a wealthy suitor, so her father shut her up in his house close by the tea-garden. Koong-Shee begged Chang to help her to escape before the peach came into blossom, and he succeeded in doing so. In the willow pattern they are seen escaping across the bridge. They were followed, alas! by the irate suitor to a distant island, where he set fire to their house. The spirits of the lovers were transmuted into doves, which are seen hovering over their old haunts.

spot, in the mellow evening light, as you could possibly imagine. A weed-covered pond, fringed by willows, surrounds the group of tea-houses, which are reached by a zigzag bridge, across which passes a ceaseless stream of blue-robed passengers: gentlemen carrying their birds out for an airing; mothers with babies in their arms, wearing gaily coloured caps surmounted by scarlet tufts; coolies with heavy loads; children dangling sundry purchases, such as a bit of meat or vegetables, from the end of a string or blade of grass—a fascinating throng to watch, if not to be absorbed into!

Close to the garden is a mandarin's palace, into which we gained admittance after much hammering. The reception-rooms were lofty and dignified, furnished only with Chinese lanterns, some handsomely carved chairs, alternating with little tables (just large enough to accommodate tea-things) set in two rows facing one another, and scrolls on the walls. The garden was entirely composed of rockwork, with the greatest possible length of pathway comprised in the smallest possible area. One of the stairways led up to a handsome summer-house with a balustrade consisting of a sinuous dragon, some forty feet long, carved in stone. Beside his gaping jaws sat a little stone frog, preparing to leap in—a good specimen of the humour which makes Chinese art so attractive. A few willows and shrubs adorned the garden, but no flowers—a feature characteristic of Chinese gardens, where design and architectural work such as summer-houses, bridges,

TEA-HOUSE IN OLD SHANGHAI

... light, as you could possibly ... covered pond, fringed by ... group of tea-houses, which ... across which passes a ... of passengers : gentlemen ... airing ; mothers with ... gaily coloured caps sur... coolies with heavy loads ; ... purchases, such as a bit of ... the end of a string or blade ... to watch, if not to be ...

... mandarin's palace, into ... after much hammering. ... lofty and dignified, fur... lanterns, some handsomely ... with little tables (just large ... tea-things) set in two rows ... walls. The ... with the ... comprised ... tiny ... con... carved ... a little stone frog, ... or the humour ... attractive. A few willows ... the garden, but no flowers—a ... gardens, where design ... summer-houses, bridges,

and walls are the most important matters. On different parts of the inner walls of this garden were stone medallions, representing scenes in the Mandarin's life.

On emerging from the garden by a different door from the one we came in at, we were confronted by a row of images, and found it was a joss (=worship) house; the few worshippers present were prostrating themselves—two at a time—before the altar, behind which stood the gods. The air was laden with the smell of incense, joss-sticks burning in a stand on the altar; and huge stone lions guarded the door. It was apparently the quietest and least frequented part of the city.

In the courtyard was a fine bronze monument, said to be over 2000 years old, round which a market was going on; the people sitting on the ground, surrounded by their wares, mainly vegetables. By way of variety there was a man with a large assortment of coal-black tresses of hair for sale, as even the poorest Chinaman is not above improving his queue with a false addition: also there was a large basket full of grasshoppers in cages about an inch square, "shrilling" at the top of their voices. From this courtyard ran a street full of shops of cooked meats. Above the counters hung split dried ducks, which looked as if they had been petrified in the act of flying with outstretched necks and wings. Below them were baskets full of eggs, black with age, preserved in a mixture of straw and lime, esteemed a great delicacy, as also seaweeds and sea-slugs—the most revolting, evil-smelling things—like fat caterpillars. Rows of little dishes contained various kinds of relishes, and there were piles of white square steamed flour dumplings, which is the Chinese form of bread.

Passing up the street, you come to a vegetable stall, the most exquisite harmony in reds and yellows; scarlet persimmons, bananas, pomeloes like yellow cannon-balls, yellow and scarlet capsicums, all sorts of nuts, a yellowish fruit shaped like a hand and called "Buddha's fingers," and baskets of dingy-coloured grapes, were some of the things for sale. Rotten pears cut in half seemed to find a ready sale; and *à propos* of pears, I must tell how a lady in Peking peeled one for my sister with her finger-nail! and how another, in describing the shocking extravagance of her neighbour, ended as a climax with the statement, "She actually throws away her pear skins!"

The next street was full of coffin shops, particularly dear to the Chinese heart, as a coffin is a complimentary gift from a son to his father. They were mostly black, and would probably be ornamented with gilt lettering; but in Canton scarlet coffins are the fashion.

Nauseous smells rose from the open gutters. Myriads of mosquitoes are wont to settle upon hapless visitors, but a solution of eau de Cologne and pyrethrum rubbed over face, ankles, and other vulnerable spots kept us fairly immune.

Leaving old Shanghai, you come into a whirling throng of carriages, wheelbarrows, and rickshas, of which there are thousands darting about. When an Englishman happens to be the occupant, the speed of the ricksha is automatically accelerated. Whole families of Chinese women and children, dressed in every colour of the rainbow, manage to pile themselves on the barrows. At the street corners stand Sikh policemen, tall handsome men with dazzling white turbans, who contrast finely with the celestials. There is a greater variety of vehicles in use here than in any other place that I have visited in the East, and they all go much too fast for the safety of passengers, considering the narrowness of the roads. The slightest push upsets a barrow. The swiftest of all the vehicles is a sort of low victoria, drawn by a rat-like pony. This is specially used by stockbrokers, who dash out of an office into it, one foot in the carriage and one on the step: they never think of sitting down, but are whisked away to another office, into which they dash like lunatics, and so on *ad infinitum*. A feverish activity seems to possess all the business population, and every movement says "Time is money." It is only in the evening that the business folk of Shanghai may be seen strolling along the Bund or sitting on the benches, which are labelled "Europeans only." Hard by is the public garden, where no Chinaman is allowed to enter—an offensive piece of insolence as long as other Eastern races can strut about in it; but it is in keeping with the attitude, unfortunately, of a large number of Europeans towards the race among whom they dwell. Not long ago a notice might have been seen, "No Chinamen or dogs admitted."

It may seem strange that the Chinese post-office is in the foreign concession, but the reason is that it is under European management together with the customs, which are under the same roof. If you wish to send off a parcel to Europe, you must first take it to the Customs House, where it has to be opened for examination. If you happen to be a lady you are shown into a division marked "Ladies only," and the Chinese officials save you all further trouble: they do your parcel up with a dexterity which makes you envious, and seal it according to regulation; and it is all accomplished with a swiftness and courtesy that might well be copied at home.

One day we drove to the fine American college of St. John's, about five miles from the city. We passed along the Nanking Road, where the most beautiful Chinese shops are. The façades are of handsome carved gilt woodwork, with balconies in which there were parties of men drinking tea. Unfortunately, these shops are gradually being replaced by European shops with plate-glass windows, and soon this part of the city will be quite spoilt. Gay carriages were following the same direction as our own, the Bubbling Well Road, and we were amused to see in one a party of Chinese girls evidently returning from school, and with their little handmaiden hanging on to the perch behind, where you would expect to see a boy in livery. Inside the carriage was a mirror and a sort of dressing-table and a flower-vase, as the custom is at Shanghai. On arrival at the college, we were taken first to see the orphanage, where tiny little creatures of about two or three years old came and solemnly bowed to us, with folded hands. The two youngest members of the establishment were babies, one of whom had been rescued from destruction. The father and mother had both been born on unlucky days, and when the baby girl had the same misfortune they utterly refused to have anything to do with it. She was accordingly taken to St. John's at two days old, and has thriven capitally. We visited successively the boys' and girls' schools, and finally were taken round the college by the principal, Dr. Pott, to whom is mainly due the great success it has achieved. There are about 120 scholars, all of whom have to pass an entrance examination in English, and they pay what are considered somewhat heavy fees, so that the bulk of the expense has not got to be met from mission funds (American Episcopal). At present the only two final schools of the college are theology and medicine, but many of the students go on to America for further college courses. We visited the dormitories, and were interested to compare the boys' belongings with those of English schoolboys. Each boy has his own teapot, and can always get a supply of boiling water. Many of them had musical instruments, some flowers, some birds, some crickets. They are fond of having "cricket matches"—that is to say, with live crickets. In winter the boys all bring hand-warmers into class, and Nelson's ink-bottles are the most approved for this purpose.

As regards games, Dr. Pott said that it was with the utmost difficulty that Chinese boys can be got to exert themselves; but they are gradually getting keener, and the average of attainment is steadily rising. On a board in the college they have a list of honours won, and this keeps up the interest. In answer to a geography examination question, "What are the five principal races?" the answer was, "Fifty yards, hurdle race, &c."! The college has a fine library, alumni hall, chapel, and playing grounds, but the laboratory leaves much to be desired. It is affiliated to an American university, and has the highest reputation of any educational establishment in China. Certainly, to judge by one of its students, who travelled with us for six months as interpreter, it is worthy of the highest praise.

Since our visit a new hall has been added to it, and there will be accommodation for another 100 students when the building is completed. The cost is being largely defrayed by Chinese well-wishers, £600 having been already contributed by them.

CHAPTER H

Shantung, the German Sphere of Influence

WE left Shanghai by steamer on October 2nd, and reached Tsingtao (the port of Kiaochow) at about 8 P.M. on the 3rd. We were grateful to be allowed to stop on board for the night, as our train started from a station close at hand at 7 A.M., and we were saved the trouble of going to an hotel. The harbour is picturesquely situated at the mouth of the bay, surrounded by hills which have all received German names since the occupation. We were up betimes, and rather disturbed by the non-appearance of the Customs House official, without whose presence we could not go ashore. However, he appeared in time to let us get to the little wayside station, and we found other passengers waiting there, seated on the line with their luggage in a haphazard way. The Germans have not only got the concession known as Kiaochow, but also thirty miles on each side of the railway line which they have built from Tsingtao to Tsinan, the capital of the province, a distance of about 250 miles, through the centre of the province.

The port is laid out just like a German town, and has hotels, statues, a post-office, commercial buildings, and private houses. The place is a fashionable summer resort, consequently the prices are high, and have gone up at least 50 per cent. since the coming of the Germans, who spend money lavishly.

The German Government has just decided to build a High School for Chinese boys of the upper class, at a cost of £30,000.

The rail is the dearest and dirtiest I have ever seen. The officials treat foreigners with indifference, and the Chinese with brutality—at least, so we heard at every place at which we stayed, and from the people who most appreciated the coming of the railway. One can only hope that things may be improved later, and a better class of officials put in charge of the line. There was but one train per day going in each direction, and the journey from Tsingtao to Tsinan takes about twelve hours. Occasional trains run on sections of the line. Although money has been poured out like water to make the German occupation a success, the object has so far not been accomplished, perhaps owing to lack of harmony between the three principal German officials in China—the Governor of Kiaochow, the Ambassador, and the Commander of the Fleet. The bulk of the trade on the line is still in Chinese hands, and the merchants have succeeded in getting permission to build a branch line from the treaty port, Chefoo, to Weihsien, which will be a great advantage to them.

Naturally the Germans, after spending so much on their port, do not like to see trade diverted to another. They not only refuse to build the line themselves, but have memorialised the Throne to prevent the Chinese from being allowed to build one either: however, their representations have failed.

The province of Shantung is considerably larger than England, and is the most densely populated of any in China—557 persons to the square mile. Although it is well cultivated and prosperous in appearance, the partial failure of the crops has the immediate effect of throwing 50,000 of the inhabitants into a state of beggary. When this happens, the Government grants each beggar daily a bowl of rice. It is hard to realise this state of affairs when you pass through such a prosperous-looking country; the crops are wheat, different kinds of millet, sorghum, maize, sweet potatoes, beans, peas, hemp, and indigo. A large quantity of fruit is also grown—pears, apples, apricots, peaches, cherries, grapes, persimmons, &c. Every now and then you pass brilliant patches of vegetables of various sorts. A villager's plot of land usually contains all the requisites of life—cotton (for clothes and bedding), wheat, potatoes, a fruit-tree, and last, but not least in China, a castor-oil plant; a few fowls and pigs will give him what most he loves in the way of food. I have known a Chinese woman eat fifteen eggs at a sitting, and she was surprised at the fit of indigestion which followed this meal! There is a curious specimen of fowl cultivated in this province, called the Cottonwool fowl; it is small, white and fluffy, looking just like a toy out of a cardboard box, and is exclusively used as medicine, especially for the diseases of women. Its flesh is dark, and the bones black; the chickens are the sweetest-looking objects. In contrast, the pigs of this part are black and hairy.

After leaving Tsingtao the train travelled slowly, stopping at every station, and these stations are all alike except a few large ones. There was a ticket office, and a row of five wooden-looking Chinese policemen standing at attention and drawn up in line as long as the train was in the station. They wear black sailor-hats, and hold batons as if they were rifles. For all the world they look like toy soldiers at 11¾d. per dozen, made in Germany. There are no platforms on these stations, and passengers squat on the line surrounded by their bedding, teapots, and birdcages. The Chinese take to railway journeys like ducks to water, so the trains are well filled. A woman may be seen approaching on her donkey, which travels at about the same rate as the train, so she stands a good chance of catching it even if she has started rather late. She is a picturesque object sitting astride on the top of her bedding, attired in a blue coat and pink trousers, tied in at the ankle with pea-green ribbons over white socks; the finishing touch of the costume being the coyest imaginable little pointed embroidered shoes.

At Weihsien, which we reached after some five

A SUBURB OF WEIHSIEN

wool fowl; it is like a toy out of used as medicine, Its flesh is dark, ans are the sweetest- In the pigs of this part are

train travelled slowly, these stations are all a few There was a ticket a row of wooden-looking Chinese standing at attention and drawn up in as the train was in the station. They sailor-hats, and hold batons as if they were all the world they look like toy soldiers dozen, made in Germany. There are on these stations, and passengers squat surrounded by their bedding, teapots, and The Chinese take to railway journeys water, so the trains are well filled. A be seen approaching on her donkey, at about the same rate as the train, so good chance of catching it even if she rather late. She is a picturesque object on the top of her bedding, in a trousers tied in at the ankle with white socks; the finishing the costume being the coyest imaginable embroidered shoes.

which we reached after some five

and a half hours' travelling, we were met by a friend, and passing out of the station, we found on the "cab-stand" a row of wheelbarrows waiting to take passengers to the town, about half a mile distant. The country is dotted with a good number of trees, mainly willows, poplars, cypresses, and mulberries, above which tower the walls of the city. We were carried in chairs, and were charmed with the view, as a lovely clear stream flowed at the base of the walls, reflecting a deep blue sky. Weihsien is an important business city, and its streets are named after the trades plied in them, such as Forge Street, Gold Street, and Silversmith Street. To us they appeared picturesque, but some people might call them squalid, and it is certainly wisest to look up, not down. We passed through the outskirts of the town to a fine-looking mission station, mainly built and worked by American Presbyterians who had recently coalesced with the English Baptists. This mission station was completely destroyed by Boxers in 1900, but now there is a fine group of buildings, including boys' and girls' schools, hospitals, a church, college buildings, and houses for workers (who number about twenty), and the whole is enclosed within a high wall. So far the teaching, even of Western science, has been entirely carried on in Chinese, but the demand for the knowledge of English is so pressing that it has recently been added to the curriculum.

From Weihsien we went next day to Tsingchowfu by rail, a journey of about two hours, and this is one of the great historical centres of the Empire. Here, again, the railway station was at a little distance from the town, and we found chairs waiting to convey us thither. The town has an imposing position on the hill, with a stream flowing round the greater part of it; consequently the walls look an astonishing height from the outer side, at least twice as high as from within, and the main entrance is across a bridge.

Within the gloomy north gate hangs a group of cages containing magistrates' boots, but it is probable that they were originally used to hold something very different, namely, criminals' heads. In *Les derniers Jours de Pékin*, Pierre Loti describes those he saw just after the siege, all with the queue hanging down between the bars.

There are many fields within the city, and if time had allowed I should willingly have stayed several weeks sketching there. The ruins of the palace belonging to the Ming dynasty are fast falling to decay, and as, unfortunately, the Government does not take any interest in the preservation of national relics,[1] it is not unlikely that they may entirely disappear one of these days.

Both here and at Weihsien we were struck with what we heard of the village girls' mission schools, showing the stability of character and also the capacity of Chinese girls. When a village wishes to establish a school, its inhabitants ask some mission to supply a

[1] A society has been formed in China this year (1908) for the purpose of preserving ancient monuments, as they are suffering not only at the hands of travellers, but of native officials.

teacher, and they make themselves responsible for the rest. The girl teacher is probably lodged in the home of the village elder, and he makes arrangements for the schoolroom, &c., and acts as guardian to the teacher. She organizes work, and has entire control as long as she manages it properly. About twice a year a missionary goes to inspect it and examine the scholars. We felt it would be interesting to see one of these schools, so our hostess offered to arrange the matter, and took us one day to the village of Wang Mu Chiang Chwang, some ten miles distant, which she was intending to visit for the purpose of inspection.

CHAPTER III

A Day in the Country (Shantung)

DAYS in early October are perfect for visiting the country. The thermometer stands at 70° to 80°. We set out one clear, fresh morning at about eight o'clock. I went in a sedan-chair, and the two others in a wheelbarrow—not such an uncomfortable conveyance as might be supposed, except when the roads are very rough. The occupants recline on each side of the wheel, and parallel to it, in a padded seat with back rests and cushions, their feet extended full length in front; the barrow is wheeled from behind, and has a man harnessed like a beast in front. As this was a heavy barrow there were two additional men pulling, one on each side of it. The sedan-chair travelled quicker than the barrow, and had the advantage of taking short cuts across the fields. It was carried by four men, two in front and two behind; the front ones carried by means of a pole, to which the shafts were suspended—which ran parallel to them—while the carriers at the back were in the shafts themselves. When the men wished to shift the weight from one shoulder to the other, they supported the pole by means of an upright one which they carry for the purpose. Owing to these arrangements the chair can be equally well carried by three men as by four, two in front and one behind, in which case the back carrier is much farther from the chair than the front men.

I was soon well ahead, and did not witness the catastrophe that happened to the barrow shortly after starting. Going round a corner rather too fast, the barrow was upset, and one of my friends was tipped out into the dust; but the other, on the upper side, managed to hold on. Happily, no damage was done, as the fall was into a soft, clean heap of dust. But it was not so pleasant a matter for another friend to whom this happened when she was travelling the same road earlier in the year. She was tipped over into a sea of mud, and as she happened to be carrying a basket full of eggs, she suddenly found herself in a "Yellow Sea."

Leaving the city behind us, we passed through open country where every one was still busy harvesting in the fields. Some fields were already ploughed, in others green wheat stood a few inches high; it would not be much higher before the snow came to cover it for winter. Much of the foliage looked more like spring green than autumn, and many of the villages lay embowered in trees—willows, aspens, cryptomerias, the last-named always belonging to temples or adjoining graves. The threshing-floors were filled with golden grain being prepared for winter storage. Bean pods were being broken up by means of stone rollers, worked by donkeys, blindfolded with neat straw goggles. On one occasion I saw a donkey wearing a pair of ornate blinkers, bright blue cotton with protuberant black eyes surrounded by a white line. The Chinese love to decorate the things in common use, and it is a perpetual joy to see the skill and ingenuity expended on simple objects. After the bean pods have been crushed the different parts of the plant are raked into separate heaps on the threshing floor—bean, husk, stalk, and chaff—for every particle is used in one way or other. If one were asked to state what was the most striking feature of this great empire, I almost think it would be this: the carefulness which prevents waste, the ingenuity which finds a use for everything. Even the green weed covering the ponds is used as fodder for pigs. When the fields look quite empty after harvest, the women and girls gather together the few remaining straws. Every inch of ground is cultivated, except the endless mounds, the graves of countless generations.

The country was a scene of delightfully cheerful energy, whole families working together; a tiny child lying naked, basking in the sun, the women (despite their bound feet) as busy as the men. Barrows passed along, groaning under loads so heavy that it needed a friend to drag in front, while at the end of some five yards of traces a donkey trotted along, waiting to give its assistance till it was more urgently needed, as, for instance, going uphill or over difficult ground. The reins were attached to each side of the barrow, and could only be manipulated by a dexterous twist of the wrists. Occasionally a man rode by on a pony, whose coming was heralded by a tinkling of bells. As the country is covered with crops, not many cattle are to be seen, and any there may be are mainly fed on bean cakes. We were swiftly borne through village after village, and my men only set me down for one ten minutes' rest during the ten miles, which we covered in two hours and forty minutes.

As we entered Wang Chia Chuang (Wang = family village), the whole community, headed by the Wang family, turned out to meet us, having been warned the day previous of our intended arrival, and we were ceremoniously led to the Guest Chamber. On the outside of the entrance to the house little strips of red or orange paper were pasted up, and in the inner courtyards as well. On these papers are sayings from the writings of Confucius, or other mottoes, such as the following:

> When you sit quietly, think of your own fault;
> When you chat together, mention not another man's.
>
> In teaching children, good must be taught;
> To win a reputation, study may be required.
>
> Diligence and frugality are the principal thing in maintaining a house;
> Humility and mildness are the boat for crossing this world.
>
> Honesty keeps the family great;
> Classics make the generation long.

These couplets are renewed at the beginning of the year, and the village schoolmaster has a busy time writing them.

Tea was brought in, and not only the family and schoolgirls, but also the neighbours came to see us, pouring out a flood of talk, of which we understood nothing. Then we went into the schoolroom across the courtyard, and found it and the girls as clean as soap and water could make them. The certificated teacher was about twenty years of age, and in this case happened to be Mr. Wang's daughter. Her room opened out of the schoolroom, and was a pattern of neatness—it was ornamented with photos. Her salary is £3 per annum. The curriculum of these village schools consists of the three R's, singing, drill, and sewing, and it is wonderful to see the difference in the appearance of the girls after they have been a short time under training, the awakened intelligence showing to a marked degree. The more promising students get drafted on to the boarding-schools for further training, with a view to their becoming teachers. The largest of these schools only contain thirty scholars, but they have two teachers for that number of scholars. An official who happened to visit one of these schools was filled with astonishment at the behaviour of the girls; as soon as he entered they all stood up, and answered the questions he put to them with modesty and clearness. He said how different this was from the behaviour in the national schools for boys, and sent a large sum of money (comparatively speaking) to be divided among the scholars, as a mark of his appreciation. In the large towns Government schools for girls are being started, but in the country

[illegible] not only the family and [illegible] neighbours came to see us, [illegible], of which we understood [illegible]. Then we went into the schoolroom across the courtyard, and found it and the girls as clean as soap and water could make them. The certificated teacher was about twenty years of age, and in this case happened to be Mr. Wang's daughter. Her room opened out of the schoolroom, and was a pattern of [illegible] was ornamented with photos. Her salary [illegible] annum. The curriculum of these village [illegible] consists of the three R's, singing, drill, and sewing, and it is wonderful to see the difference in [illegible] of the girls after they have been a short time under training, the awakened intelligence showing [illegible]. The more promising students get drafted on to the boarding-schools for further training, with a view to their becoming teachers. The largest of these schools only contain thirty scholars, but they have two teachers for that number of scholars. An official who happened to visit one of these schools was filled with astonishment at the behaviour of the girls; as soon as he entered they all stood up, and answered the questions he put to them with modesty and clearness. He said how different this was from the behaviour in the national schools for boys, and sent a large sum of money (comparatively speaking) to be divided among the scholars, as a mark of his appreciation. In the large towns Government schools for girls are being started, but in the country

E.G.K.

there are only mission ones. Dating from the new year (1909) school attendance is compulsory for boys throughout the Empire, therefore the Government is responsible for the establishment of the requisite number of schools—at least one in every village. At first there was a difficulty in starting village girls' schools; now they are in great demand, and sufficient teachers cannot be obtained.

After we had heard the children sing and had inspected their writing and sewing, &c., we watched Mr. Wang doling out medicine in a patriarchal way in the courtyard. Several people had taken the opportunity of our visit for killing two birds with one stone, namely, seeing foreigners and obtaining medicine. One of them showed us her unbound feet with great pride, as she had just achieved the process of unbinding, and she presented us with her old shoe, much worn, but beautifully embroidered, in which she used to work in the fields. The Chinese naturally have remarkably small feet, and in this village most of them are unbound, as the majority are Christians, but the feet are so tiny that in many cases it is difficult to believe that they are not bound. The women wear white linen socks, and their wide trousers are neatly fastened over them with different coloured braids. Village life here looks eminently patriarchal. The sons do most of the work, all living with their families under the same roof. One of the daughters-in-law had a beautiful Madonna-like face, as she sat nursing her baby, with other youngsters crowding round her knees. No one could have failed to admire the saintly expression and graceful pose. The two married daughters of the house were living in a neighbouring camp with their husbands, who are Manchu officers. All the prefectural towns have Manchu garrisons, but it would not be possible for a foreigner to tell the difference between Manchu and Chinese soldiers.

Our visit came to rather an abrupt close, as we were warned that we must reach the city before sundown or the gates would be closed. Mr. Wang brought in preserved pears and tomatoes strewn with sugar, which are esteemed a great delicacy, and then we started on our homeward way. Work in the fields was ended for the day, but for many of the Chinese work is never ended. Until all the grain is housed, watch must be kept by day and night. Small huts are erected in the fields for this purpose, sometimes perched on tall poles, from which a wide outlook can be kept over the country, or on the threshing-floors adjoining the farms.

CHAPTER IV

Shantung Silk

THE next morning we pursued our railway journey as far as Chowtsun, but we had great difficulty in getting tickets. Before leaving Shanghai we inquired at the bank what sort of money we should take for Shantung, and were told that notes would go everywhere, so we accepted what the bank gave us. On the railway they demurred at every place where we offered notes, and at Chowtsun they absolutely refused to take them. In vain I expostulated in German. The Chinaman pretended not to understand. Nothing would induce him to say a word or give us tickets, but he said in Chinese that he must have Mexican dollars. Finally, we left the office, and when the train arrived we had our luggage put in, and got in ourselves. The man came out of his office, and looked surprised. He then poured forth a flood of German. I told him that he would be reported for incivility at the station to which we were going, and where we would pay for our tickets. He had evidently imagined we should be intimidated and should produce the dollars. Chowtsun is a charming place, and we found plenty of the now fashionable

Shantung silk to be bought there, but much finer in quality than one sees in London shops. We were taken to look at it in an inner room, and provided with tea. The merchant said that the Shantung silk blouse which I was wearing was very poor quality, and he showed us some lovely stuffs, all hand-woven. On the counter were lying Manchester cotton goods, which are imported all over the Empire. It is interesting to learn that Shantung has been noted for its silks since 2640 B.C. In the Chinese classics of that date silk is referred to as being made in the south-west of the province, where the mulberries grow well.[1] At the present time the silkworms are fed on dwarf oak in the eastern part of the province, and pongée is made from their silk; but all the finer silks come from the west. From the time of Yu (who flourished B.C. 2640) there is continual reference made in the classics to sericulture. A later writer says that in his time it was forbidden to rear more than one breed of silkworms in a season, because astrologers had discovered that horses and silkworms belonged to the same constellation, and therefore must be of the same origin. Later on, in a classical book of the Han dynasty (B.C. 204), the ceremonies connected with it are described, and how the Empress herself took part in it, none of her ladies being allowed to wear jewelry when picking mulberry leaves to feed the young insects, and "none dare indulge in indolence"; "lewd

[1] The first Chinese settlers are said to have come from the shores of the Caspian Sea, bringing with them the silkworm and the mulberry.

conversation" was said to disturb the worms. From this time onwards it appears that successive empresses had to take a ceremonial part in the rearing of silkworms. Silk was the most interesting product of the province to us, but the main interest of the country to others lies in its mineral worth. The Germans have got mining rights, and have carried a branch line of the railway down to the coalfields at Poshan.

From Chowtsun we went on a barrow, through interesting country, to the town of Tsowping to visit a friend, and as the roads were good we quite enjoyed our four hours' ride. Specially careful barrowmen had been selected, so that we might run no risk, and certainly this was desirable, as the path often lay along the edge of steep banks. We found a good mission hospital up there, where we heard astonishing stories of the recuperative powers of the Chinese. The Scotch doctor said that when he told them to his friends at home, one would remark, "I am not a bad liar myself, but I would not dare to go so far as that." My own experience at a hospital in China makes me think that it is impossible to beat the reality, no matter how exaggerated the story sounds!

From Tsowping we returned by barrow to Chowtsun, and thence by rail to Tsinan, which boasts three railway stations.

The accompanying illustration gives an idea of what is worn by officials. The self-complacent pose of a Chinese official's feet is eminently characteristic. Much has been written about character as seen in the human hand, but I think a character study of feet might still be written, even when the feet are disguised by boots or shoes.

OFFICIAL (COURT DRESS)

ch. iv

nently characteristic.
character as seen in
a character study of
even when the feet are

CHAPTER V

Tsinan

THE capital of Shantung is a large city, containing a population of about 150,000 inhabitants. Tsinan is a city of real beauty, owing to the fact that there are bubbling streams in all parts of it, so that the trees grow well. The water is singularly bright and sparkling, and looks attractive even in the dirtiest gutters. As it comes bubbling up in every direction there is a radiance about it which seems untarnishable. In the very centre of the town is a temple, standing on a terrace with fine carved balustrades round it, in front of which is a large pond full of this bubbling water, overhung by willows—a typical Chinese picture. On the other side of the pond is a busy market, whence crowds soon collected round us to watch our sketching and photographing. They were quiet and polite, and it was quite unnecessary for the policeman to come and keep them at a distance. But then that manœuvre gave him the advantage of an excellent view for himself! Everywhere we found a Chinese crowd of spectators preferable to one composed of Europeans. The market interested us greatly, having every kind of ware for sale, from rags and silk scraps, out of which elegant shoes are made, to all sorts of weird medicines, of which the emblem was a life-sized, double-headed fowl, planted in the centre of the counter. Hard by the medicine stalls was an enclosed space, where a woman was telling a story to an interested crowd. The professional story-teller is quite an institution here, as elsewhere in the East, but it is rarely that a woman is seen in that capacity. In fact, women take but small part in the business life of the country, and men do all the selling in shops.

Not far from the market, but situated on the outskirts of the town, is the University, a recent institution (1902), and built mainly in European style; the professors' houses being of two stories and entirely un-Chinese. The entrance, however, is the usual native one with carved and painted woodwork decorations; facing it, and crossing a little bridge over an empty tank, was the guest-room, supposed to be purely Chinese, but full of European lapses, in the shape of lace curtains, wall-papers, European carpet, chairs, clock, electric bells, and, most striking of all, a centre candelabra for the electric light. There are lecture-rooms, libraries, museum, laboratory, and dining-rooms, and thirty-two baths with hot and cold water laid on; these are so popular that their use has had to be limited. Amongst the institutions may be named a fife and drum band, and the latest novelty is a brass band. The University is only open to the students of the province of Shantung, and naturally the standard of Western knowledge is still low; but there are professors of English, German, French, and Japanese, though the respective numbers of their classes are seven, five, five, two. At present Japanese is not so popular as it used to be. Indeed, in the Imperial College in Kaifeng the Educational Board has just cut out Japanese: whether this is an exceptional case I cannot say.

The English section includes a study of European history (Freeman's) and political economy, but other subjects, such as geography, are popular among students, to judge by their use of the small English library. Curiously enough, the most popular book both here and elsewhere is "Little Lord Fauntleroy." Half the lectures are devoted to Western knowledge and half to the Chinese classics, and the course of study at present covers three years.

In connection with the scheme of education, and under the same jurisdiction, are normal schools, secondary and primary schools. One of the principal ones has an English headmaster, so that there will soon be a set of students prepared to profit much better by university training, and fitted to go to some European university later. There are no fewer than fifteen schools and colleges, with about two thousand five hundred students. Another interesting feature of the education question is the opening of a girls' school for the daughters and wives of the officials. It was built three years ago by two Chinese gentlemen, and they have an English teacher there. The school was formally opened by the Literary Chancellor, and on entering he saluted the girls deferentially, and gave them an admirable address. In the south of China many ladies learn reading in private, but in the north this is extremely rare, and so lately as 1902 there was not a single girls' school in the Empire, except the mission schools; now they are cropping up in all directions, and the Government is taking an active interest in all their concerns. Possibly it may be thought that it shows this in somewhat exaggerated fashion, for a recent order has been issued from the Education Department in Peking prohibiting the wearing of a long fringe of hair, or "bang" as our American friends call it, in any of the girls' schools throughout the Empire. This fashion had become rather general last year. It would have been of much more practical value if all scholars had been forbidden to paint, as this is one of the most time-wasting processes. At Tsinan the school hours have been obliged to be fixed late because the scholars require some hours for the morning toilette. In the girls' schools they are now very anxious to learn English, music, and drawing; "accomplishments" are more valued than serious study. It is quite evident that there is no lack of ability to learn, though the girls are called "wooden-heads" sometimes in contempt. In the American Board School at Peking the girls gave an admirable rendering of Wagner's and Mendelssohn's music in part-singing. The piano is also very popular among the girls. Like the boys, they have astonishing memories, and think nothing of reciting a whole Gospel; it is even not ranked as a feat by the Chinese to know the whole of the Bible by heart.

Tsinan is a most progressive town: it has a British postmaster, who has organised, not to say revolutionised, the postal system of the province. Letters now go to Peking in four days, and to Tientsin in three and a half days; the runners carrying them reckoning to do fifty or sixty miles at a stretch, with an average speed of three and a half miles per hour. They receive about five shillings a week as wages. Sir Robert Hart is responsible for the selection of postmasters, and even in a remote place we found a very nice one who could speak a little English. Sir Robert Hart was appointed head of the Customs Department in 1862, and the Customs and Post-Office form part of one system.

One of the prettiest places at Tsinan is the lake, the main pleasure resort of the Chinese. After threading our way in chairs through incredibly dirty and narrow lanes, filled with a jostling crowd and traffic, often brought to a standstill by a hopeless-looking *impasse* of rickshas, barrows, beasts, and chairs, we came to a gateway, and stepped thereout straight on to the edge of the lake, where boats, with graceful latticed-work windows, and a broad couch to lie on in the front, awaited passengers. Tea was ready on the table, and we set off along one of the water highways through the tall reeds and beds of lotus. Gorgeous kingfishers darted to and fro like a flash of light; tiny wild-ducks bobbed up out of the water, and then scuttled into the reeds, as we slowly made our way to the various points of interest. The lake has been chosen as a place for putting up memorial monuments to distinguished people, and they are certainly a singular contrast to ours. They stand like temples on little islands, and to the uninitiated appear to be such, with their tablets of incense and altars. For instance, there is a fairly recent one erected in memory of a former Governor of Shantung. Above the altar, and almost hidden by the inscribed tablet, is a life-size seated figure of the Governor. The head is a photograph, and the rest is a painting, but in the dim light it required close inspection to ascertain this fact. Incense is offered before it by any one, and not only by the members of his family, as in ancestral worship. Opposite this building, and as part of the memorial, is an ornate theatre, where plays are acted on public occasions. Another recent memorial has been put up to Li Hung Chang, and it is extremely strange. It includes a little summer-house and a rock-garden (without rock-plants), a theatre, a house containing a tablet, altar, &c., and a guest-house where distinguished visitors can be lodged. This last building is two-storied, and quite European in style, perched on an elevation with a well-built wall below it, surmounted by barbed wire. Another little group of buildings had corrugated iron walls; on another was a Taoist temple, where we found a travelling showman who was exhibiting a popular cinematograph in the neighbourhood. The Chinese frequent the lake for pleasure parties, and a good deal of drinking goes on, not of tea only. A visit by moonlight is as enchanting as anything that could be imagined. On one of the islands we noticed the most fascinating of all the fascinating birdcages we had yet seen. It was the usual round shape made in bamboo, but the centre of the roof inside was a well-executed portrait of the handsome, black talking bird which inhabited it. The seed- and water-pots were of different colours and shapes, and fastened in with tiny figures of men carved into wooden buttons. I have never been in any country where there were so many caged birds, and where they were so well looked after. Every cage has its well-made night-cover, and often this is fastened down the side with neat little buttons. We continually saw men carrying cages along the streets, taking their birds for walks, as we do dogs. At one place we saw a man take the cage to a stream, and after he had cleaned it out with a sort of tooth-brush, he left it in the stream for the bird to have its bath, after which he hung it up to dry, and whistled to the bird. The fashion of carrying birds about is said to be for the purpose of showing that the owner is a man of leisure; as this is now creating a good deal of ridicule, the custom is likely to go out of fashion.

One of the interesting sights of Tsinan, which is quite up to date, is a large camp, lighted by electricity, about two miles outside the city. It is built like rows of little cottages ; the men are well drilled, and have to attend lectures. We found them, when they acted as our military escort through the province, very civil, and in every way pleasant and obliging men. A party of them was brought by an officer to visit the mission museum, and the men were much interested in having the various kinds of natural history and geological specimens, models of architecture, electrical machines, steam-engines, &c., explained to them. Visitors are surprised to see a model of an English cemetery, but it throws a new light on English character when the Chinese receive an explanation of our views with regard to the dead, and the care lavished on their last earthly dwelling-place. Models are of great value when wisely used for dispelling misconceptions, but we are often prevented by our insular pride from taking the trouble to disabuse foreigners of false impressions they may have conceived of us. One of the most attractive models is a dredge worked by electricity, for the province of Shantung suffers terribly from the inundations of the Yellow River, and the means used to cope with this difficulty are wofully inadequate.

This museum was originally started by Mr. Whitewright, of the Baptist Mission at Tsingchowfu, where the prefectural examinations used to take place, attracting to it 10,000 or more students from all parts of the province. When the old examination system was abolished the city of Tsingchowfu was no longer of importance from this point of view, and it was decided to move the Institute to the capital, Tsinan, a treaty port whose importance, on the other hand, was rapidly increasing. The Mission obtained an excellent site, and put up a lecture-hall to seat six hundred persons, reception-rooms for men and for women, a reading-room, and the museum. The first block of buildings was opened in 1905 by the Governor, and ever since then the place has attracted an increasing number of visitors of all kinds. In the second year of its existence there were 187,000 admittances; at the great annual religious festivals it is specially crowded, as thousands of pilgrims pass through Tsinan on their way to the sacred mountain, Tai Shan. From 8.30 A.M. till 6 P.M. preaching goes on without intermission, a specially selected staff of native preachers assisting the missionaries in this work; for the Chinese prove themselves more able than Europeans to win converts to Christianity.

Many of the students from the university and the schools frequent the museum and lecture-hall, the walls of which are hung with charts and diagrams calculated to give the thoughtful Chinaman much food for reflection. After studying the comparative tables of commerce, population, &c., a visitor is said to have exclaimed, "Why! the *only* thing that China is ahead in is population!" Lectures on history, science, and religion are given in the hall, and are largely attended by university students on Sunday, as, in imitation of our Western custom, they have no classes at the university that day.

One day a week the museum is open to ladies only, and we met the wife of the retiring Governor of the province just leaving the building after an exhaustive examination of its contents. She was accompanied by a considerable retinue on horseback and in chairs, not to mention a motley crowd composed of the rag-tag and bobtail of the town, carrying absurd little flags.

It has now been decided to attach a medical school to the Institute, as there is none in the province, and a church is also to be built. The American Presbyterians and the English Baptists are combining for this medical school. The former society has had medical work here for the last twenty-eight years, and for many years they have had a hospital and dispensary in the eastern suburb. There is also a free dispensary in the city, a Government affair, where the patient is at liberty to choose either Eastern or Western treatment. The majority choose the latter, and are treated by a German naval doctor ; they are indebted for his services to the German Government, who have lent him for this purpose. There are already classes for medical students in connection with several of the mission hospitals in the province, who will form an excellent nucleus with which to start the new college. The importance of medical mission work in China is great, not only for its own sake, but also for the purpose of familiarising the Chinese in the most remote corners of the Empire with the benefits of Western science and the goodwill felt towards them by Europeans and Americans, of which this is the practical demonstration. The two continents are about equally represented, and there are over three hundred doctors scattered throughout the Empire: their fame extends far beyond the limits of the neighbourhoods where they happen to be residing. They are training numbers of intelligent young Chinamen to carry on their work, but the establishment of colleges to complete the training of these students is now becoming increasingly necessary.

The work already achieved by medical missionaries in China is by no means small or unimportant. They form an association, by means of which the task of fixing the terminology of medical science has already been accomplished. They have published a standard dictionary in Chinese, as well as the latest American and English text-books on this subject. The Chinese medical student, therefore, is not entirely dependent on oral teaching, if he has no knowledge of English. Another branch of this work is the organised labour of their research committee. The geographical distribution of disease, the various forms of it prevalent in different districts, and the methods of treatment come under this heading. Men of undoubted ability and with the highest medical qualifications are engaged in this work.

The Chinese Government has recognised the value of what has been already done by its official sanction of the Union College at Peking—the first attempt made in China to give a full medical education.[1] The late Dowager Empress contributed to its initial cost, and the Government has pledged itself to grant degrees to the students who have successfully passed its examinations. There are about seventy to a hundred students in it at the present time.

This is a somewhat long digression, but I think it will not be without interest to readers to have a general idea of the scope of medical mission work in China at the present time.

There is an arsenal near Tsinan, where an English officer, who had just been allowed to see over it, told us they seemed thoroughly expert, and able to reproduce anything they tried. They were busy making locks for a canal, and less than a hundred miles away we passed another large arsenal where they were busy making ammunition. The smoky chimneys were quite suggestive of home!

The most interesting feature of our stay at the capital was an interview with the Governor of the province, to whom we had an introduction. His Excellency Lord Wu is an intellectual-looking man, but worn and bowed with age. He had granted us an audience one afternoon, and on our arrival at his *yamen* (=official residence) we were led through a circular doorway in the wall, into the gardens, in which were little ponds and bridges, and an arbour made in the shape of a boat. We waited the Governor's coming

[1] Five missionary societies have combined to provide a good teaching staff. It is to be hoped that several other such union colleges may be established in different parts of the Empire.

in a summer-house, a terrible European erection, furnished with a crimson and " Reckitt's blue" plush sofa and revolving chairs to match. On the table were glasses and plates, with proverbs inscribed round them, and cups of the type seen at a Sunday-school caterer's. Cake, champagne, and tea were set out on a parti-coloured table-cloth, which was ornamented with a florid design in chain-stitch composed of every colour of the rainbow. His Excellency soon made his appearance, accompanied by an exquisite-looking interpreter who spoke English well—better than he understood it, I fancy. For nearly an hour he plied us with all sorts of questions as to my education (he had been much exercised by F.R.S.G.S. on my Chinese visiting-card), occupation, our past and future travels. He not only gave us good advice with regard to our journey, but practical assistance—as we afterwards discovered—by sending word to the magistrates on our route through the province. An interested but somewhat ragged audience watched us from the doorway, and the Governor's personal attendant played with his queue, but somehow nothing could disturb the dignified impression of the old man. He had known Gordon, and at the time of the Boxer troubles he had sent the missionaries safely out of the province, in direct opposition to the orders he had received from his Government. He is a strong, good man, and I much regretted that our conversation had to be carried on through an interpreter, for that process is paralysing to thought, not to mention that one had grave doubts as to the accuracy of the interpretation. The interview lasted about an hour, and was terminated by His Excellency inviting us to drink champagne or tea, after which he escorted us back through the garden to our chairs.

CHAPTER VI

The Sacred Shrine of Tai Shan

SHANTUNG is the most interesting (historically) of all the provinces in the Empire, and we determined to visit two particularly sacred spots which were not far from the capital—Tai Shan (one of the four sacred mountains of China) and Küfow, the home of Confucius.

We started on a beautiful autumn morning, with quite an imposing cortège. First came our mounted military escort, then ourselves in two light mountain chairs, each carried by two men and with two to relieve them. Next came the cart, with our interpreter (a minute person clad in khaki, boasting the name of Fergus Summer—though a Chinaman), the cook, some baggage, and the men's bedding. Finally a mule brought up the rear, carrying our baggage, some one's bedding, and our other servant perched cross-legged on the top. It was a delightfully exhilarating day, and not less so the thought that we were really beginning our adventures off the beaten track, and had said good-bye to the railway for at least three weeks, to try far pleasanter, if slower, means of transit. The chairs were light frames with a hanging foot-rest, quite comfortable when padded with our bedding, and with an awning fastened on light bamboo rods above us. We were well manned, so we comforted ourselves as to the fact of their carrying us between twenty and thirty miles a day by remembering that they were only too pleased to get the job. They were pleasant, cheery fellows, with fine mahogany-coloured backs, and did not seem the least bit jaded at the end of the day's march. They go lightly clad, the most solid part of their clothing being the pig-tail curled round their heads. The rest of their garments were well ventilated, and sometimes seemed in danger of falling to pieces altogether. Their food seemed most inadequate —a chunk of bread, an onion (alas for the passenger who hates the smell of an onion !), endless cups of tea at wayside restaurants, and frequent whiffs of smoke from their tiny pipes. They are wonderfully good-tempered, always ready for a laugh, and most attentive and careful for one's comfort.

The first day passed without any adventure, but was pleasantly spent in charming scenery, and we passed a somewhat uneasy night trying to accustom ourselves to our new beds (light camp mattresses with an air pillow under the hips—an excellent arrangement) and strange surroundings in an inn. It was an easy task to get up early next day, and we started at 6 A.M., so as to do a four hours' stage before breakfast—fifteen miles. The country was full of interesting sights : one hamlet we passed through seemed to have a monopoly of whips ; every shop was full of

MOUNTAIN CHAIR

with our bedding, and with an
... bamboo rods above us. We
... we comforted ourselves as to the
...ing us between twenty and thirty
...membering that they were only too
... job. They were pleasant, cheery
...ogany-coloured backs, and did
... bit jaded at the end of the day's
... clad, the most solid part of
... the pig-tail curled round their
... garments were well venti-
...seemed in danger of falling to
...food seemed most inadequate
... onion (alas for the passenger
... an onion!), endless cups of tea
...nd frequent whiffs of smoke
They are wonderfully good-
MOUNTAIN CHAIR ... for a laugh, and most attentive
...mfort.

... without any adventure, but
... charming scenery, and we
...y night trying to accustom
... (light camp mattresses with
... hips—an excellent arrange-
...roundings in an inn. It was
...arly next day, and we started
... hours' stage before break-
... country was full of interest-
... one ... passed through seemed to
monopoly ..., every shop was full of

them and of nothing else. In another plaited straw for hats was the only article for sale. Farther on, we came to a district where each village had large bunches of maize hanging in golden clusters from the trees, looking like fruit. As we turned a corner into a deep gully we came into a bevy of barrows in full sail—like a fleet of blue-sailed boats—bearing down upon us. They were the only ones we saw, as there was not much wind, but it was an unforgettable sight.

As we approached the city of Tai An we were met by a fine soldier in red plush breeches, but the rest of his costume was not to match! He had come six miles from the city to act as our escort, and told us of a noted Buddhist temple that we must stop and visit. There was an extraordinary seated gilt Buddha, with a broad grin on his face, and another grave one standing, but there was nothing particularly noteworthy, as far as we could see. The soldier told us that preparations had been made for our entertainment at the inn, but we had arranged to stay with a hospitable American lady, who had lived out here for over fifty years, and as soon as we arrived she sent to engage chairs to take us next day up the holy mountain. Chinese books say that it has been the holy mountain of the East for the last 4000 or 5000 years; it is certainly one of the most frequented to-day, and at the usual times of pilgrimage (February and March) as many as 10,000 will go up in a day. Most of the pilgrims go up on foot, a few on their knees, and the wealthy ones in chairs.

We started betimes in chairs—there is a special guild of chair-bearers, and they are simply wonderful—they are called "climb-mountain tigers," and as soon as they saw my size they demanded an extra man. I was quite willing to comply with the demand, though they would not have suggested it to a Chinaman of twice my bulk! It was a lovely morning, worthy even of such an expedition. We were carried about two miles across the fields before we came to the foot of the mountain, and from there to the top the way is well paved or made in flights of granite steps, some ten to twelve feet wide, up to the top of the mountain. There is even a well-built wall of cut stone on either side, the cost of this road being defrayed (as well as the upkeep of the temples) by the gifts of worshippers. The road was not very steep at first, and was lined by houses, where no doubt a profitable trade is plied by the sellers of paper money, shoes to be presented to the goddess P'i-Hsia Yuam-Chun, incense, and "light refreshments." There are many temples on the mountain—in fact, there seems to be one every few yards—but we had not time to spend in visiting them; and we set our faces to walk up a large part of the 6600 steps which lead to the top. It took us some five and a half hours to climb up, and as we neared the Gate of Heaven (the pink gateway in the sketch) the steepness grew, the last flight being over 1000 steps (I counted them), most of which were so narrow that not more than part of the foot could be accommodated: the steps

ful
as
tra
de-
to
ly

ere

to

oad
les)
ery
ubt
per
Isia
iere
iere
ime
; to
l to
; to
(the
the
m),
han
teps

chairs—there is a special ... they are simply wonderful ... mountain tigers," and as ... they demanded an extra ... to comply with the demand ... would not have suggested it to ... my bulk! It was a lovely ... of such an expedition. We ... miles across the fields before ... of the mountain, and from there ... well paved or made in flights ... ten to twelve feet wide, up to ... tain. There is even a well-built ... either side, the cost of this road ... well as the upkeep of the temples) ... worshippers. The road was not very ... lined by houses, where no doubt ... plied by the sellers of paper ... presented to the goddess Pi-Hsia ... , and "light refreshments." There ... on the mountain—in fact, there ... very few yards—but we had not time ... them; and we set our faces to ... of the 6600 steps which lead to ... us some five and a half hours to ... neared the Gate of Heaven (the ... sketch) the steepness grew, the ... 1000 steps (I counted them), ... so narrow that not more than ... be accommodated: the steps

were much higher than they were wide, so that it was more like a ladder than a staircase. Heavy iron chains were suspended at the sides for the worshippers to drag themselves up by, and a Chinese woman with us went up on all-fours. The way towered above us in contrast to the "Peaceful Mile," a shady part of the road lower down; but it was very lovely, with its scent of wild thyme, fragrant grasses, and yellow chrysanthemums. Earlier in the year it is bright with violets, forget-me-nots, and honeysuckle, and the cypresses and pine trees give great dignity to the landscape. We followed the rocky bed of the stream, which becomes a brawling torrent after rain. We only halted for half-an-hour on our way up, and the "tigers" did their work well. After we had passed through the Gate of Heaven we came on to a comparatively flat piece of tableland with thatched cottages, which might have been a Scotch moor. On the top were several temples, one to Confucius, in which was a replica of his big statue in the temple of Küfow; another to Yu-Huang, the Taoist Emperor of the Sky, who first drained the Empire; and—most sacred of all—a rough block of granite, said to have been erected there by the conqueror Ch'in Shih-Nuang.

The great Emperor Shun (B.C. 2255–2205) is said to have visited Tai Shan, "where he presented a burnt offering to God and sacrificed to the Mountains and Rivers." Certainly he could not have selected a better spot for the purpose: from the summit you look down upon a vast expanse of hilltops, like the waves of the ocean, and the lovely shining rivers below wind away like silver threads between them. This represents the oldest form of worship in China, existing before the rise of Taoism, Confucianism, and Buddhism. The earliest sacrifices are said by Chinese writers to have been organised by Fu Hsi, nearly 3000 years B.C. His successor built a temple for the worship of God, where sacrifices were offered to the mountains and rivers. This was followed by the worship of the sun, moon, and five planets, and there are traces of this still to be found in Chinese Buddhism, which has incorporated so many alien ideas from other religions.

The great sacrifices to God and to earth were offered at the winter and summer solstices by the Emperor: he also sacrificed to the four quarters and to the mountains and rivers of his Empire. The nobility sacrificed each to their own quarter, with its rivers and mountains. The royal sacrifice was a young ox of one colour, which had been specially reserved for the purpose. The sacrifices of the people varied according to rank and to the season of the year —a bull, a ram, a boar, scallions and eggs, wheat, fish, millet, a sucking pig, unhulled rice, a goose.

The sacrifices in early times consisted of meat and drink; those offered to heaven were burnt, and those to earth were buried, accompanied by the beating of an earthen drum. But sacrifices were not very frequent; in the "Book of Rites" it says: "Sacrifices should not be frequently repeated. Such frequency is indicative of importunateness ; and importunateness is inconsistent with reverence. Nor should they be at distant intervals. Such infrequency is indicative of indifference, and indifference leads to forgetting them altogether. Therefore the superior man, in harmony with the course of nature, offers the sacrifices of spring and autumn. When he treads on the dew, which has descended as hoarfrost, he cannot help a feeling of sadness which arises in his mind, and cannot be ascribed to the cold. In spring, when he treads on the ground, wet with the rains and dews that have fallen heavily, he cannot avoid being moved by a feeling as if he were seeing his departed friends. We meet the approach of our friends with music, and escort them away with sadness, and hence at the sacrifice in spring we use music, but not at the sacrifice in autumn" (Legge's translation).

Such a poetic description of worship is worthy of the scene which greeted our gaze on the mountain after we had passed through the Gate of Heaven, the fine culminating point of the steep ascent. The view from the summit, which is but a gentle ascent from the Gate of Heaven, was absolutely glorious—range upon range of mountains, countless villages dotted over the forty miles of plain and in the folds of the hills, and above all the winding, shining river, going away, away, away, till it was lost in infinite space. Was it that the effect of such a vision unhinged the minds of worshippers, since this became the place where people cast themselves down into the abyss? There were so many deaths that the authorities have had it walled in, and the place is called "Cliff of the Love of Life."

When we began our descent we resolved to do the correct thing—despite the terror it inspired in us—and be carried down the almost perpendicular stairway. The men carry the chairs sideways, because of the narrowness of the steps, and run down, pitter-patter, as hard as they can go. I had my watch in hand and timed them—a thousand steps in six minutes. The most horrible moment was when they flung the chair, with a dexterous turn of the wrist, from one shoulder to the other. One false step and we should all have been killed together; but the "tigers" never make a false step. Really the only danger is that the carrying poles may snap. The whole return journey—reckoned at thirteen miles—took only two and a half hours. The height of the mountain is 5500 feet, whereas Tai-an is only 800 feet above sea-level. Stones are carried from it to all parts of the province, and when a house is built with an unlucky aspect—namely, facing a cross-road or a turning—one of these stones is built into the wall, with an inscription, "The stone from Tai Shan accepts the responsibility."

CHAPTER VII

The Home of Confucius: Küfow

THE next morning we were just about to start, when the magistrate of the city was announced (imagine a ceremonious call at 7 A.M. !), and he was ushered in, together with his present to us—a tray containing fine pears, pomegranates, dates, and nuts. We accepted part (in Chinese etiquette this stands for "gratitude for his generosity"), and returned part ("humility of the recipient"). He was immediately served with tea and cakes, and explained to us that, owing to a message from the Governor of the province, he had been expecting our arrival and had prepared an inn for us. Understanding that we were just setting out on our journey, he only stayed a short time after we had thanked him for his hospitality, so that we were able to do our day's stage in good time.

The following day we started at 6 A.M., and managed our thirty-six miles in twelve hours, as the roads were in good condition. At midday we halted for lunch at an inn, where we were told that the magistrate had made preparations for our entertainment. A scarlet curtain was hung in front of the door; there were mats and carpet on the floor of the two rooms, coverlets on the *khangs* (=brick bedsteads), a good table and European chairs, scrolls on the walls, a white table-cloth, and, to complete all—a champagne lunch! We declined the champagne, lager-beer, and most of the "plats," but enjoyed the chicken and eggs. The advantage of having the inns cleaned up and fresh mats put down is great. Our military escort, varying from one to four, is highly diverting, and they are usually mounted on shaggy ponies, on which they look quite fine, especially when they have their scarlet or yellow umbrellas up.

As we approached our destination, Küfow, a man came dashing across the plain at full gallop, and flung himself off his horse at our feet, announcing that the magistrate had ordered a private house in the city to be prepared for our reception, to which he would conduct us. Just outside the gates we found four soldiers standing at attention: they gave us a military salute, bobbing down till their right hands touched the ground and then emitting a startling yell. Accompanied by them (they remained with us in attendance till we left Küfow) we soon reached our quarters, a characteristic Chinese gentleman's house, very nice and clean, in which a suite of three rooms was placed at our disposal (the block seen in the sketch). A major-domo received us at the entrance and led us ceremoniously to the inner courtyard, where tea was at once served, and we were told that dinner would be ready shortly, and that the magistrate would call on us as soon as we had dined.

PRIVATE HOUSE: KÜFOW

PRIVATE HOUSE: KÜFOW

Our interpreter, Mr. Summer, had informed us that he was the son of an official and knew exactly what ought to be done ; so we placed ourselves in his hands, and our visiting-cards and thanks were at once despatched to the magistrate. After dinner the chairs were arranged in rows, and tea and cakes set on the table in readiness for his arrival. He asked particularly if we had enjoyed our dinner, which he had ordered to be cooked in European style, and it was quite good and palatable, especially as we had the best of sauces after our long day's march. It appeared that our host had provided three cooks (trained in European ways), three other servants, four soldiers, and two policemen to look after us, but our own men undertook all the personal attendance.

Next morning we went in procession to the temple—the Holy of Holies of Confucianism—for all the establishment seemed to think they should accompany us. We decided to make a détour in order to approach it from the most picturesque side, and the view was certainly charming as we walked along the moat outside the city wall, where lotus leaves floated on the still water, and tall rushes and flags rustled under the leafy trees. Nothing was needed to enhance the beauty of the spot, and a few minutes' walk brought us to the celebrated avenue of cypresses leading to the south gate of the city, within which is the fine entrance to the temples. They are enclosed in a park which occupies a whole quarter of the town, and has plenty of trees to form a worthy setting for the large groups of buildings connected with Confucianism, temples not only to Confucius but to his parents, followers, and to the other great sages, Mencius and Yentzu. The buildings are some of the finest in the Empire, and very lofty, with their double-storied roofs covered with orange and green tiles. The eaves are heavily decorated with fine coloured woodwork, protected with netting from the vast flocks of birds and bats that hover round them, and the pillars of the Hall of Perfection are magnificently carved monoliths. In the first courtyard are many interesting stone tablets, eight or ten feet high, standing on the backs of stone tortoises or mythical beasts of similar shape in picturesque little temples with yellow-tiled roofs and Venetian red woodwork. Hoary cypresses towered above them. In the next courtyard was a preaching hall (not in use for that purpose, however), from which we ascended by a long steep flight of stairs, with folding gates half-way up, to a dark upper chamber. Another flight of steps took us to a room surrounded by a balcony, from which we had a splendid view over the many temples clustered round a great central one, which appears above the orange and green tiled temple in the sketch which I took from this point of view. It is the most imposing of the group of buildings, and is entirely tiled with orange, none but Confucian temples being allowed to have this colour. Flocks of crows, pigeons, and other birds were circling round it; indeed, we had been awakened by the deafening noise they made in the early morning. In the courtyard as well as in the

CONFUCIAN TEMPLE

temples were fine old bronzes ; carved marble steps led up to the principal hall, a lofty building with pillars and red painted woodwork. Here Confucius sits under a canopy, with handsomely embroidered curtains partly shrouding him, and an altar bearing bronze incense bowls in front. On either side, at right angles, are the figures of two other great Chinese sages, Mencius and Tze-Sze, seated in shrines, and behind them again are six disciples seated against the walls on either side.

The sacrifices to Confucius were formally established by an emperor (A.D. 59), who also ordered that the teaching of Confucius should be studied in all schools throughout the Empire. This is still done everywhere, even in the new universities, but the actual sacrifices—pigs, sheep, and cattle—are reserved for temple worship. These take place before dawn in the second and eighth month. There is plenty of room in the grounds belonging to the temple for pasturage, even for the vast number of animals required, as it is about 8000 acres in extent. More than 500 years elapsed after the death of Confucius before he was universally worshipped, but the worship had the royal sanction, for his teaching is aristocratic in character, whereas that of the yet greater but less noted sage, Mencius, was as thoroughly democratic.

Confucianism is rather a system of ethics than a religion. Confucius merely accepted (and that only to a limited extent) the religion of the age and country in which he lived, and he added to it a code of morals dealing largely with the government of the State. He said, "I am not an originator, but a transmitter." Confucius lived contemporaneously with the Buddha, but no two great teachers of mankind could have differed more widely from one another than did these, both in character and in teaching. In the Buddha, love and pity for the sorrows of humanity drowned every other feeling, and he resolutely refused to use his powerful intellectual faculties for any other purpose than to lessen suffering, and eventually to rid the world of it. Confucius, on the other hand, allowed his intellect free play, and it appears to have led him to look with tolerance, and a certain measure of acquiescence, on the religious beliefs of the age. There is a famous saying of his, "Respect the spirits, but keep them at a distance." At the same time, he was conscious of his mission as a teacher sent by God; he says, when threatened by the people of K'uang: "After the death of King Wen, was not wisdom lodged in me? If God were to destroy this wisdom, future generations could not possess it. So long as God does not destroy this wisdom, what can the people of K'uang do to me?" Confucius seems to have been a superstitious man; he was apt to turn pale at a thunderclap, and he sanctioned the practices of the village folk for driving away evil spirits.

The most important features of his teaching are the high ideals which he inculcated for the ruling of the State, and the stress he laid on the obligations of men to their fellow-men, even more than on their obligations towards God. One of his fundamental doctrines was that all men are born radically good. This doctrine is not accepted—at all events, at the present day—with regard to women ; the Chinese would be more inclined to say, " All women are born radically stupid," or, as the women themselves frequently put it, " We are only wooden-heads." Confucius also strongly advocated the duty of reverence and sincerity, and " protested against any attempt to impose on God." He rose from his seat in the presence of any one dressed in mourning. The five cardinal virtues taught by Confucius are righteousness, benevolence, politeness, discernment of good, and sincerity.

It will be readily understood from the above brief account of Confucianism that it is quite possible to combine it as a religion either with Buddhism or Taoism, and in point of fact it is not unusual for a Chinaman to profess all three religions at the same time, or by turns. I was told in Shansi that sometimes a village would feel aggrieved at their gods not having protected them from some disaster, or given them sufficiently good crops, so they would decide to try another religion for a time. The transformation in a village temple is easily effected.

Not only were divine honours paid to Confucius, but his family also were promoted to places of honour in the cult, and had adjoining temples raised to them, though only his father was granted a statue. In one of the temples is a fine series of stones engraved like brasses, descriptive of the life of Confucius. These are so greatly admired that it has been found necessary for their preservation to have papers pasted across them intimating that rubbings are not to be taken from them. Some of these tablets are fine specimens of writing—for Küfow is above all places the home of Chinese literature—and the inscriptions aim at being brief, telling, and enigmatic. Their value depends also on beauty of style and calligraphy.

The temples are only about two hundred years old, as they have twice been destroyed by lightning. The first time it happened, a thrill of terror ran through the whole Empire: nothing further happened, so the next time the nation took it quite calmly. There are no priests to look after the place, and, to judge by its neglected appearance, the five families exempted from taxation by some bygone emperor, in order that they might devote themselves to the care of it, have become extinct. The emperor used formerly to come at stated times in order to offer sacrifices, as being the visible head of Confucianism, but now he contents himself with sending every two or three years to decorate the temple and keep it in repair.

As we were leaving it began to rain a little, so the soldiers and police put on their hats, till then slung on their backs: when it rains heavily they put up the scarlet umbrella as well!

After lunch we called on the magistrate to thank him for his hospitality and to take leave of him, attended by all our retinue, plus the rag-tag and bobtail of the town, with our card-case (measuring $11\frac{1}{2}$

CEMETERY OF CONFUCIUS

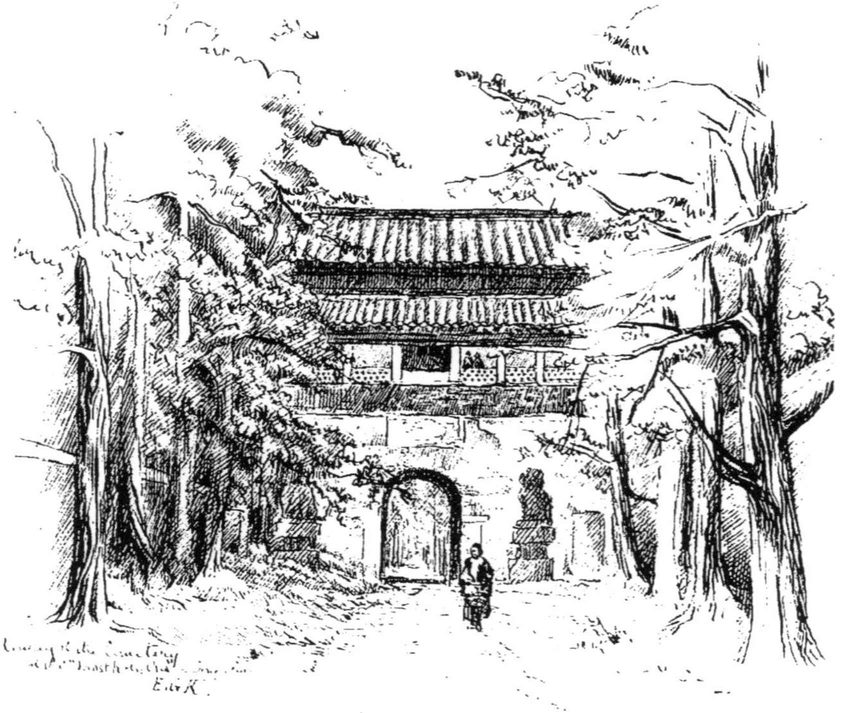

inches by 6½ inches) carried in front by the servant; then came "Mr. Summers," who had managed to raise a horse for the occasion. Tea and cigarettes were handed round, and we were placed in seats of honour on a sort of platform. We did not linger, as we were anxious to complete our pilgrimage by visiting the grave of Confucius, situated in a park a short distance outside the town. It is approached through a series of gateways of varying sizes and importance. Long avenues of cypresses lead from one gateway to another, and at last a spot is reached from which every one is commanded to approach the grave on foot. This is simple and dignified, as befits a sage—nothing but a tablet bearing an inscription, set up on a plain low pedestal, shaded by trees. Near it are the graves of other members of the family of Confucius, which are much less modest. His grandson's tablet has two curious tall stone figures of servants on each side. This descendant wrote a celebrated treatise called the "Doctrine of the Mean."

In the evening the ladies of the family of the official to whom the house in which we were staying belonged asked permission to call on us. We entertained them and asked all the polite questions we could think of, such as their names, where they came from (Chinese officials always seem to be moving about the country), number of children, their age, &c., and we were asked similar questions in return. Suddenly a hitherto silent member of the party asked in a shrill tone, "What is your rank?" a most difficult question to answer so that they could understand, except in an ambiguous way. They were much pleased to drink " English " tea, which is quite different from what is prepared for the Chinese market, and to eat English cakes, some of which they carried away in their handkerchiefs.

The following morning we took our leave, hoping that our guide would prove his official skill by correctly tipping the various members of the establishment, and the same ceremonies were gone through as on our arrival. The guide sent the cook to " buy cash," which was carried after him, as he felt far too important to carry it himself. The money worry was beginning to grow acute, as its value varies every day, and at Kŭfow we found two complete systems of coinage in use, one reckoning only half as much as the other; the 100 cash meaning anything between 80 and 97, but never by any chance meaning 100. The Government, not to mention banks and officials, reckons to get a " squeeze " out of everything, so it is lucky that money is subdivided into infinitesimally small values; 100 cash being worth about twopence-halfpenny.

On leaving Küfow we took a somewhat different route from what we did in coming, as we wished to visit a Buddhist monastery, and again we were entertained by hospitable magistrates on the road. Evidently they have found former travellers thirsty for something else than the national beverage, so Münchenes Bier was provided. On the second day we had a long stage—38 miles—to do, so we got up at 4.30. Alas! No sooner were we ready than down came the rain, in a most uncompromising way, and the men refused to set out. After waiting a couple of hours it seemed to be clearing; we made a feeble start, but the men crept along like snails, and their steps were so uncertain on the slippery ground as to make us quite nervous. We got safely across the ferry, though the water had risen a good deal considering how little rain had fallen. Our soldier escort galloped away under his red umbrella, and we saw him no more. The men set us down in an inn doorway on the farther side of the river, provided themselves with hot sweet potatoes from an itinerant vendor who happened to be passing, and refused to go any farther in the rain. By dint of persuasion and the promise of sixpence each extra (exorbitant sum!) if they would do the stage that day, we got them to make a fresh start. We plodded slowly on for five hours, and found we had done twenty miles by the time we reached our midday rest; we halted for an hour, and the rain stopped, so that we got on much better afterwards. During the rain there was not a creature to be seen except ourselves in all the wide landscape, but the minute it stopped the people appeared in every direction as if by magic. In the village streets we found great difficulty, as the rain had converted them into one big puddle, and the men tried to hop about from stone to stone. When it grew dark we were terrified, and I clutched a large cider-down pillow in readiness to cover my face when I should take the seemingly inevitable plunge into the morass. However, we escaped all disaster, and the men walked without stumbling through dry water-courses and over rough boulders, and the cart jogged along over impossible places. When the moon rose it was like fairyland ; and at eight o'clock we triumphantly trudged into our inn.

The following morning we started at six o'clock for the celebrated Buddhist monastery of Lu, and reached it about 11.30. This monastery is situated up a solitary valley about six miles from the high-road, and the situation was splendid. It nestled in a hollow of lofty hills, its tall pagoda standing out sharply from the trees. There was a pylon part way up, and two stone bridges with yew-trees overarching them. The buildings round the temple are not at all imposing, but the entrance gate has a gilt Buddha seated in the centre, surrounded by four huge statues, each of a different colour, representing tutelary deities belonging to the Taoist religion ; and back to back with Buddha was another god.

The first temple we came to contained three seated Buddhas with a curious rockwork background, but beyond it and up a flight of steps was a much more imposing temple, of which both design and colouring were a facsimile of what we had just seen at Küfow, only on a smaller scale. It was impossible, judging by the exterior, to tell that it was Buddhist and not Taoist or Confucian, but inside there was no mistake.

MOUNTED MILITARY ESCORT

Our escort
Oct 19. 1907

Buddha sat enthroned on a large lotus blossom, with a halo behind him and a thousand little seated gilt Buddhas on shelves all round the hall. Life-size figures of the 42 Lo Han were seated against the walls, and amongst them were the two emperors, pointed out to us by one of the monks. We discovered for ourselves a figure who we felt sure was Marco Polo : he had the face of an Arab and wore a drapery over his head, unlike any of the other figures ; the monk could only tell us that he was a man from the West. What would Marco Polo have said if he could have foreseen that he would be placed among the Buddhist " holy ones"?

The rest of our journey back to Tsinan was accomplished safely in two and a half days.

CHAPTER VIII

The Yellow River and Grand Canal

WE had little difficulty in deciding which route to take from Tsinan to Tientsin, as the railway journey to Tsingtao and by ship thence were both equally disliked by us. We determined to strike across country (travelling in the same way as to Küfow) as far as Tehchow on the Grand Canal, and to go up it by boat to Tientsin—in all, a week's journey. The country is flat and not nearly so varied as the rest of the province, but it contained one most interesting experience for us, the crossing of the Yellow River. When we reached its banks we saw a far more turbulent flood than that of the Yangtze, and of the same dull mud colour. It took a little time to arrange for us to be ferried across and then to get our cart and mules on board, and we had time to study the route to be taken, as there was a large amount of traffic at this point. It seemed strange that there was no bridge across, especially when we saw the difficulty of navigating it; but it may be that, as the river is so capricious in its choice of a bed, the authorities consider it not worth while to build a bridge. The enormous amount of silt and mud which it brings down with it soon fills up the bed and causes frightful inundations. Dikes have to be built, and when they are broken through by flood a most extraordinary method of repairing them is used. A sort of gigantic pad of earth and stones, in a basket-work made of *kaoliang* (=sorghum) stalks and roots, is prepared and lowered into the breach by means of ropes, thousands of coolies being employed on the task. None but Chinese could devise or manage to execute such a work. On one occasion over 4000 people were drowned by the breaking down of a dike. Now the Government is seriously considering how to deal with the difficulty of controlling the course of the river. When we were safely on board the large ferry-boat, the boatmen towed us up the river-bank for about half-an-hour till we came to a point at which we could start, and then they came on board to row. It taxed their powers to the utmost, and by dint of straining every nerve they landed us at a point just opposite to that from which we originally started. Their work looked the most arduous I have ever seen.

In the year 1852 the Yellow River took a new course (which was still further changed in 1887) from the south of the province of Honan, in a north-east instead of a south-east direction, so that now it falls into the Gulf of Chili instead of into the Yellow Sea, to the south of the province of Shantung. Its present mouth is some three hundred miles distant from its former one. It has with good reason been named "China's Sorrow." Like the Yangtze, it rises in the mountains of Tibet, and follows a devious course of 2500 miles through northern China ; but unlike the Yangtze, the main highway of commerce, the Yellow River or Hwang Ho is of no use for trade purposes. A decree has just been issued granting ten sticks of great Tibetan incense to be burnt at the altar of the Dragon King Temple (riverine deity) in token of Imperial gratitude because there was a peaceful river last year. This is done in response to the report of the Governor of Chili ; and rewards have been given to a number of officials for their vigilance in connection with the Yellow River conservancy.

The following day we wanted to visit an American hospital a little more than a mile off the high-road to Tehchow, and had no end of difficulty in first persuading the men to permit the visit and then in finding the road. We decided to let "Mr. Summer" and the luggage go straight on to Tehchow, to get arrangements made for the boat, the kind Irish postmaster at Tsinan having sent word to his subordinate there to get us one. We progressed but slowly, asking every creature we met which was the way. The Chinese peasant is a stolid being, doing his task and taking little account of anything else, but at last we did arrive, and spent a couple of hours seeing school, hospital, &c. The result of our slow progress in the morning was that we did not reach Tehchow till it was pitch-dark, and by mistake our men were not told to go to the post-office for "Mr. Summer," while we waited at the mission-room of the people whom we

OUR HOUSEBOAT, GRAND CANAL

had just visited. In vain we tried to make the servant understand, and the evangelist's household was equally uncomprehending, but kindly brought us tea. After much consultation over our affairs they fetched a young man who spoke English beautifully, and he at once set about finding "Mr. Summer" and getting food for us. He was a student from Peking, and asked what we should have done if no one had been found who knew English, and after a short time "Mr. Summer" and the postmaster turned up. They had been hunting for us outside the city, and somehow had missed us in the dark.

Next morning we went on board the house-boat, and had a comfortable but somewhat tame journey up the Grand Canal, which hardly comes up to its name. I spent nearly an hour sketching our house-boat in the rosy light of sunrise before the men were ready to start; certainly the spot was not very picturesque. This was by no means the first canal to be made in China, though it is the one best known to Europeans. I shall venture to quote at length an interesting description of a much earlier canal from a paper read to the China Society in London by H. E. Lord Li Ching-Fong, the Chinese Ambassador[1] to our own Court: "Once during an inundation in China artificial channels were cut in order that the nine rivers might carry all the surplus water to the sea. Even mountains were tunnelled for the purpose of constructing canals. Henceforth the ground was cultivated again and the

[1] H. E. is a nephew of the late Li Hung Chang, and was adopted by him.

havoc was avoided. To the sagacity of Yew we attribute the merit of this undertaking, which we regard as one of the most remarkable works of man. It was begun in 2283 B.C. and ended in 2272 B.C." The Grand Canal was begun in the thirteenth century, and is over 2000 miles long, but where we entered it it is really a small natural river, and we were either towed or rowed most of the way to Tientsin, with not much assistance from the sail. It was formerly used for the transport of grain (the imperial tribute), but since 1900 the sea route has been used instead, and the value of the canal decreases daily, owing to the continually increasing facilities of transport, both by rail and by sea. We passed many villages, but only one of the forty-one cities which lie on its banks. On the fourth day we came to the custom-house outside Tientsin at 9 A.M., and asked "Mr. Summer" to inquire if we could not go by ricksha to our destination, as that would save time. He came back with the information that it could not be done, so we resigned ourselves to wait. Afterwards we learnt that it is *always* done, and that it would have taken us less than an hour to go by ricksha or steam tram, and saved us six hours of passing through the dirtiest conceivable waterway, which our noses told us was the sewer of the town! It is impossible to describe the disgustingness of what we saw, really quite the nastiest thing in China, and one could only feel thankful that at least a good deal of the native quarter had been destroyed during the siege.

Tientsin is one of the most Europeanised towns of China, and it is not only an active commercial port but is the centre of the Chinese educational movement. This was vigorously and successfully organised by Yuan Shih Kai. He made a complete system of primary and secondary schools for both sexes, and besides the middle schools there are special schools of engineering, languages, medicine, &c., including a medical training-college for women, with a well qualified Chinese lady doctor at the head of it, who was trained in America.

There is also an excellent Anglo-Chinese Mission College, founded in 1902, of which Dr. Lavington Harl, M.A., D.Sc., is the principal. Last year the students numbered 320, of whom sixty were boarders and the remainder day scholars. The curriculum now includes full training for chemical analysts and a school of electrical engineering, while it is intended to open a law school during the current year, 1909. Yuan Shih Kai gave evidence of his broad-mindedness by contributing 6000 taels to the building fund of the last block, opened in 1907. Some of the students have found this college an excellent preparation for school life in England.

Tientsin is the first city in the Empire to boast of municipal government on Western lines, and for this also Yuan Shih Kai is responsible. The Chinese are a wonderfully law-abiding people, and it is only necessary to look at our neighbouring port of Wei-hai-wei to see a remarkable instance of this. With an area of 285 square miles and a population of 150,000 inhabitants, a force of fifty-seven native police and three English inspectors is found quite sufficient to keep perfect order.

It can be no matter for surprise that Tientsin is now to be made the capital of the province of Chili instead of Paoting-fu, a city of much less importance under the changed conditions produced by recent events.

Here we took leave of "Mr. Summer," having already made arrangements for another Chinaman to go with us from Peking to Burma.

CHAPTER IX

Journey into Shansi in 1893

I NOW must go back to my first coming to Tientsin in 1893. From Shanghai I came in a coasting steamer, and it was after starting that I made the rather disconcerting discovery that I was the only woman on board. Nevertheless it was the pleasantest voyage I ever had, as my cabin had a proper bed in it and its own bathroom, and I made the happy discovery that Chinese servants could be the best in the world, while the officers all conspired to amuse me. The voyage lasted a week, and the slow passage up the mouth of the Peiho (*ho* means "river") was quite a new experience. We ran into the soft banks pretty frequently, and they crumbled like dust; sometimes we were in imminent danger of carrying away a hut as well, but happily that did not occur. One dreadful object kept recurring again and again—a tall pole on the river-bank with a basket on the top, containing a criminal's head.

At Tientsin I was met by one of my sisters and her husband, who had come to take me into Shansi. The European town was very dull and prosaic, and the native city abjectly squalid, but now the former is well laid out and there are plenty of large houses, shops, schools, colleges, and tramways. I was not sorry to get away from it, however, as I was anxious to see the real China, and we soon got our things accommodated in a small house-boat to travel up the river to Paoting-fu. Three little compartments were all we had, but we spent a good part of each day walking on the banks and admiring the lovely autumn colouring of the rushes. On my return a year later we were not so fortunate, as the war with Japan was in full swing, so that the country was too disturbed for us to walk about, and we had to take whatever could be got in the way of a boat, namely, one infested with cockroaches and other vermin. For three days and nights we sat in misery, scarcely able to eat or sleep, and when we opened our trunks at Tientsin we found them simply swarming with cockroaches. They had eaten all the straw of a bonnet, leaving nothing but lining and trimmings!

At Paoting-fu we left the river, and I had a mule litter while the others rode. These litters are the most horrible invention, as the mules perpetually tumble down, and even though you pad the sides with your bedding you get much shaken. When we came to a river we had to ford it or be ferried across, for there are no bridges in this part, and often the rivers are very dangerous. On the roads we met long strings of camels carrying packs, the tail of one animal being attached to the nose of the one behind. They have inns of their own, being cantankerous beasts, and are

CAMEL INN

supposed to travel at nights, because of being such an obstruction to traffic. Certainly if you lie awake you can generally hear the tinkle of their bells. They are a most attractive feature of the landscape in the north, whether seen in the streets of Peking, or on the sandy plains of Chili. My sketch was taken in the summer when the camels were changing their coats, so that the one in the front has a grey, dishevelled look, corresponding with Mark Twain's description. He says that camels always look like "second-hand" goods; but it is clear that he cannot know the fine stately beast of North China.

The road leading to Taiyüanfu—our objective—was always thronged with traffic, men on foot, on horseback, in chairs, or in carts. The official messengers wore yellow, and dashed along faster than any one else; but one day we met six mandarins in four-bearer chairs, carrying an important document from the Emperor at Peking into Szechwan, the western province. They were received everywhere ceremoniously, and crackers sent off in their honour; they were accompanied by a military escort and gorgeous banners.

At nights we often had to put up in wretched inns. The cold was extreme at this time of year (November), and the brick bedsteads were heated from underneath by a fire. This was all very well if it was properly regulated, but sometimes it was allowed to get too hot, and then you woke to find yourself baked like a biscuit. The nights were short, for we often arrived after dark and had to get up at 4.30. Even then it was difficult to get the men started at six, sometimes only at seven o'clock. The clear cold moonlight mornings were very lovely, and I was glad enough to walk to keep warm.

One day my brother-in-law made a détour to visit a village where there is an interesting Christian community, whose history is a remarkable one. It was the home of a thief, who in his wanderings happened to go into a mission hall and heard the story of the life of Christ. The next time he returned home, amongst other items of news he retailed what he could remember of this strange story, and so deeply interested the listeners that they found his knowledge far too meagre to satisfy them; they decided to send two of their most respected seniors to learn more about it. These men went to the mission station, were carefully instructed and became Christians. They returned to their village in course of time, taking a supply of Christian literature, and thenceforward they have given themselves entirely to the work of evangelisation *at their own cost.* Occasionally a missionary goes round to see them—as in the present instance —but otherwise they work steadily and successfully, without any assistance from Europeans. This is an example of a fact which holds good in China generally, namely, that the people do not leave mission work to be done only by the missionaries, but become the best workers themselves when they have accepted Christianity. What Mr. James (of the Bombay Civil

Service) says of the work of the Presbyterians in Manchuria exemplifies this same fact: "Of 600 people who have been baptized since Mr. Ross came to Manchuria, not more than a dozen owe their conversion primarily or chiefly to the foreign missionaries; the others have become disciples of these converts, and this spiritual seed has produced within a dozen years the sixth or seventh generation." This is the experience of workers throughout the Empire, and was expressed by a Chinese lady visiting England in a pathetic appeal for more missionaries: "If only you will send us teachers *now—for a few years*—we will do the rest."

To return to our narrative, my brother-in-law brought the two Chinese elders with him when he rejoined us on the road, and they greeted us like old friends, with radiant happiness. It was inspiring to see their simple, heartfelt piety and their absolute realisation of Christian brotherhood. We chanced to come across them again a year later on my return journey to the coast, and again I saw their simple, joyous faith, the sincerity of which could not be doubted by the most cynical sceptic. It was the one bright spot in an otherwise very trying and anxious journey, for the country was much disturbed, owing to the war with Japan, and one of our party was ill with fever—a boy of seven—and growing daily worse, so that when we at last reached Tientsin he had a temperature of 107°.

When we approached the province of Shansi we

got into a hilly district, and crossed several ridges called "the Heavenly Gates." In some cases the ascent was pretty steep (2860 feet), and there were temples at the bottom where the coolies prayed for a safe journey up. When I stopped to sketch it aroused much interest, and spectators always treated me with respect. It was explained to them that I desired to show my mother the beauties of their country, so I became the type of English "filial piety"!

The dangers of the road are numerous, and crossing the rivers is often a very perilous proceeding: sometimes it is possible to ford them, but the river-beds are so changeable that it was usually necessary to have the guidance of experienced men. Sometimes we had to be carried across on men's backs, and it is not altogether a pleasant experience to cling on to a bare, greasy back in a kneeling position, with your arms round a most unwashed neck! Sometimes we were ferried over, which was much the safest and pleasantest way of crossing, and the charge is infinitesimally small.

Another danger of the road arises from the nature of the soil, which is largely a loess formation. The road runs through deep gulleys, often over 100 feet deep and quite narrow, but the loess walls are apt to give way, especially after rain. One day we were walking quietly along under a high cliff, when a deafening thunderclap close behind us made us start and look back, to see a dense cloud of dust where the cliff had fallen right across the path we had just traversed. We had a very close shave that time. About a year later my cousin was killed by the similar breaking down of a road alongside a river; she was riding in a cart, and was buried under it in the river. A friend who was with her had just got out to walk a little, and consequently escaped.

During the rains travellers are often drowned by the sudden rush of water down the gullies, and there are places of refuge in the high banks—little caves or hollows. In some of the villages where we had to stop the night the houses were dug in these cliffs, and were really caves. The smells were atrocious, as there was but little ventilation. The chimneys form danger traps to the unwary traveller walking along the top of the cliffs; he may easily step into one, if he is not looking carefully where he is going.

The day before we reached Tai Yuänfu, the capital of Shansi, we stopped at a mission station in the charge of a delightful, courtly old Chinese evangelist, whose hospitality I enjoyed several times. He treated us royally, cooking dinner for us in European style, and would have been sorely grieved had we offered him any remuneration. When the troubles came later, not only he but every member of his little flock —forty-one in all—were "faithful unto death," refusing to accept life at the price of recantation.

The journey from the coast took altogether a fortnight, and I was glad when at last we reached the wide plain in which Tai Yuänfu is situated. In May it is a vision of loveliness with its crops of millet, sorghum, and poppy—white and puce colour—but now it was one monotonous expanse of dust. The dust storms which blow across the plain are terribly trying; they are as bewildering and as blinding as a fog, and they sometimes go on daily for weeks during the early part of the year.

Shansi is one of the worst provinces of all as regards opium-smoking, and the poppy is largely cultivated. In the accompanying sketch a group of patients is seen, who have come to a mission refuge to try and break off the habit. They are allowed to smoke tobacco, but are mostly resting or sleeping on the khang; the brick bed seen in every inn and in most private houses. On the floor in front of it is seen a small round aperture, where the fire is fed, which heats the whole khang. The present Governor of Shansi is taking active steps to put down opium cultivation, and the prospect seems hopeful. Revenons à nos moutons. When we reached the city gate there was a slight delay, as carts are apt to get jammed in it. Though the gateway is large it is considerably blocked by stones, set up by a former governor to prevent carts of above a certain gauge from entering the city: this was to encourage the trade of the wheelwrights. Now there is a railway right up to the walls of the city, but from what I have already said it will be easily understood how difficult a task it has been to construct a safe line. The railway joins the Péban line at Cheng Ting.

OPIUM REFUGE

CHAPTER X

Taiyüanfu

TAIYÜAN is surrounded by a lofty wall, with a gateway at each of the four points of the compass. The Chinese always use these terms when we should use "right" and "left": they speak of the position of furniture in a room, for instance, as being north, south, east, or west, and can always tell you the relative positions of places and things in that way. It is the seat of the Government of the province, and was the first place in the Empire to have a Western university after the 1900 troubles.

The finest of all its temples—whether Confucian, Buddhist, Mohammedan, or Taoist—is the temple of Heaven and Hell. The entrance is magnificent in colouring, with roof and walls covered with turquoise-coloured tiles peculiar to this province, which make its temples so much more beautiful than those in the west. There are interesting but repulsive statues within, mostly depicting the torments of hell. In one temple, however, there is a deity to which childless women especially come to pray. She is a hideous figure about life size, with a gaping mouth, into which they stuff raw eggs by way of offering. On the adjoining wall is a fresco representing people receiving babies out of a cash-bag full of them, which a man carries over his shoulder.

I visited the temple at the time of a large fair, which was held in its courtyards (a common custom in China), and had one of the teachers in attendance, to his great disgust, as it is not the correct thing for Chinese *ladies* to go to fairs, and European manners had not yet penetrated to this part of the Empire. It was a very fine sight, notwithstanding the absence of the élite, for the women and children were most gaily attired—and then the setting ! They were all perfectly civil to us and ready to talk. A woman was feeding her five-year-old baby, not yet weaned. Family parties kept arriving on donkeys, and women had their feet tied up in bags to protect their dainty shoes from the dust of the road. At one side theatricals were going on, to a loud and ceaseless accompaniment of drums. The theatres are all connected with the temples, a visible sign of their origin in the East as well as in the West ; and the theatre and temple dues are collected together. Actors are looked down on, and none is allowed to compete in the literary examinations ; they are in the lowest grade of society. The accompanying sketch gives some idea of the beautiful colour scheme of temple and theatre eaves. It is the open-air stage of a theatre at Showyang, about sixty miles from Taiyüan. The little figures of beasts on the roof are a characteristic feature.

THEATRE STAGE

THEATRE STAGE

The stalls were full of interesting objects from all parts of the province, and we went round buying various things that took our fancy. There were handsome embroideries and lovely silks, and I was surprised to find that we could take whatever we liked without paying for it; it was sufficient to say, "Come to the mission hospital to-morrow and the doctor will pay." No Chinaman could have had better credit, and few, I think, as good, in this city.

From the temple of Heaven and Hell we returned past the barracks, and saw the men practising walking on stilts; apparently that was part of their drill, as finally they all filed off into the yard on them. The soldiers are quite a decent set of men, and one of the officers frequently sent them to the hospital to be broken of the opium habit. It is terribly common here. In a neighbouring town it is estimated that 90 per cent. of the population (men, women, and children) are smokers.

From Taiyüanfu we made an interesting little excursion to a place to the south-west called Tsinssu, where there is a magnificent old temple on the rocky hillside dominating the village. The temple is overshadowed by hoary trees, and has remarkable golden dragons twisted round the pillars of the façade. In the grounds are hot springs, and the water flows under an ornamental bridge leading to the terrace on which the temple stands. Had it not been for the hot water it would have been impossible to sketch, as the water froze on the surface of the paper, and every few minutes I had to put my paint-box in the stream to thaw the coating of ice formed on the colours. The subject, however, was so charming that I could not waste the one chance I had of sketching, and in the afternoon I made a rapid drawing of a pagoda, with the little bells hung on each story tinkling in the breeze; an adjacent tower looked precisely like an English church, but its real use was as a granary. The hot springs are valuable in enabling the people to grow rice, which is not grown elsewhere so far north, and it is the motive-power of many paper-mills in the district. In a recent expedition roe-deer, leopards, boars, and David squirrels have been found in this neighbourhood, but we saw nothing more interesting than a beautiful pastoral scene—a shepherd lad piping a melancholy ditty to his sheep under the clear blue sky. I should like to have sketched him, but the shadows were already lengthening, and we had to hasten our return before the city gates were closed.

We attended a review one day, and saw the old régime in its full glory, now already a thing of the past. We started at 7 A.M. in the cart, and although the parade-ground was only a quarter of a mile away we were none too early. The soldiers were already mustered, and two gorgeously arrayed officials were seated in state under a canopy waiting for the Governor, with a fine sort of helmet on a stand behind them. He arrived shortly after we did, and although there was a drizzling rain the numberless banners looked

PÀGODA

lovely, bowing down while the Governor passed, and then floating proudly up again. Many of them were pale-blue silk and carried on long bamboo rods. There were a good many soldiers mounted on smart ponies that scampered along bravely; but the black turbans surmounting the blue or red uniforms made them look rather like women. Some of them were armed with bows and arrows, slung on their backs; others had prehistoric guns which required two men to work them, one to hold and the other to fire off by means of a lighted stick of incense, which at other times was thrust (lighted) into the soldier's chest, where also he carried his powder!

One regiment was a great contrast to the others—the celebrated tiger braves. They were clad cap-à-pie in yellow cloth striped with black, even the boots and cap being of the same material. The latter was most cunningly made, with little pink-lined ears which stood erect, and ferocious black eyes, and white fangs, and a red tongue hanging out. This alarming costume was supposed to render all further equipment unnecessary, and I asked one of the "braves" if he had no weapon, on which he showed me merely an ordinary knife stuck in his waistband. I asked if he would sell me his uniform, but as he could not do that he lent it, and I had an exact copy made. On my return home Mr. Chamberlain saw it, and was struck with the idea that the braves scared away the enemy by their uniform and their roaring, and made a telling use of it later on in describing the tactics of "the opposition"!

Yet a step farther back in history, it is interesting to learn how the soldiers used to travel in earlier times. A model has recently been constructed (by Professor Hopkinson) of the chariot used to convey eighteen soldiers. This chariot was in use about a thousand years ago in China, and registered distance, a gong sounding at the end of every "li" (about one-third of a mile), and a bell at the end of every ten "li." This vehicle was called the "measure-mile drum carriage," and it is from the description of the mechanism given in the writings of the period that the professor has made his model. An ode was written in its honour. The chariot was drawn by four horses.

The main features of the review were the sword exercises, varied with turning somersaults, the charging of soldiers with two-pronged pikes, accompanied by roaring—and various feats of horsemanship. The men rode about clinging to their horses from underneath, or jumped on them going at full gallop. The review lasted all day, and we got tired long before it was over. The military examinations of officers were on the old lines, and success in getting promotion depended on the *strength* shown in drawing a bow, or lifting a weight. Two officers came to hospital for treatment on account of having overstrained themselves by their exertions, and were anxious lest they should be disqualified in consequence. Now every-

TIGER BRAVE

thing is changed. There are military colleges springing up, where everything is modelled on the military systems of the West, and students go in increasing numbers to Europe to study these at first hand. The Ministry of War has decided to adopt the same gradations of rank as those of the British army and navy respectively; thus a second lieutenant in the navy will be of equal rank with a senior lieutenant in the army, and so on. In the past, military service was one of the two only ways in which it was possible in China to climb the social ladder.

In September 1904 I saw one of the last great triennial examinations, to which students came from all parts of the province. It opened with a great procession, headed by the Governor and examiners who had come from Peking. Some of the big men rode in chairs, preceded by scarlet umbrellas, and boys carrying boards enjoining silence, many banners and discordant drums. It seemed as if all the rag-tag and bobtail of the city had been collected to grace the occasion; they were decked out in magenta felt hats and scarlet cloaks which by no means covered their rags and dirt. Some wore scarlet and gilt, others green and gilt caps, but no shoes on their feet. The three principal men were carried on chairs, raised on little platforms and covered with yellow rugs, supposed to represent the imperial dragon. The imperial letters were carried (wrapped in yellow cloth) across the shoulders of men on horseback, and the imperial seals under gay canopies. The examination buildings are extensive, and are well seen from the city wall. There are 10,000 cells, arranged in rows of 100 each in alleys closed by a door. Each cell is about 6 feet high, 4 feet wide, and 5 feet deep, and is provided with a sliding seat and a board for writing on, which the student can slide into the same groove as the seat to curl up on at night, for he has to spend three days and nights without leaving it. The cell is open in front, and an invigilator walks up and down to see that no cheating goes on. If the student is taken ill he may not leave, and if he dies (not an infrequent occurrence at examination times) his body is simply put over the wall at the outside end of the alley. These examinations are competitive, and there may be only thirty or forty vacancies for thousands of students. At Canton there are 25,000 cells in the examination hall, and each province has its own examination, to which students of other provinces may not come. There are characters at the end of the rows of cells, drawn from one of the classics, which are used as numerals, to distinguish the rows from one another.

It is interesting to observe what supreme importance is attached by the Chinese to learning and to morals. Learning is the main road to eminence; the only other one—the military service—is quite subsidiary. The highest grade of the people is the Sze, the scholar, and from it all public servants are drawn. There is no bar to prevent men of other grades passing into this class, provided they fit themselves to do so and pass the

OLD EXAMINATION BUILDINGS

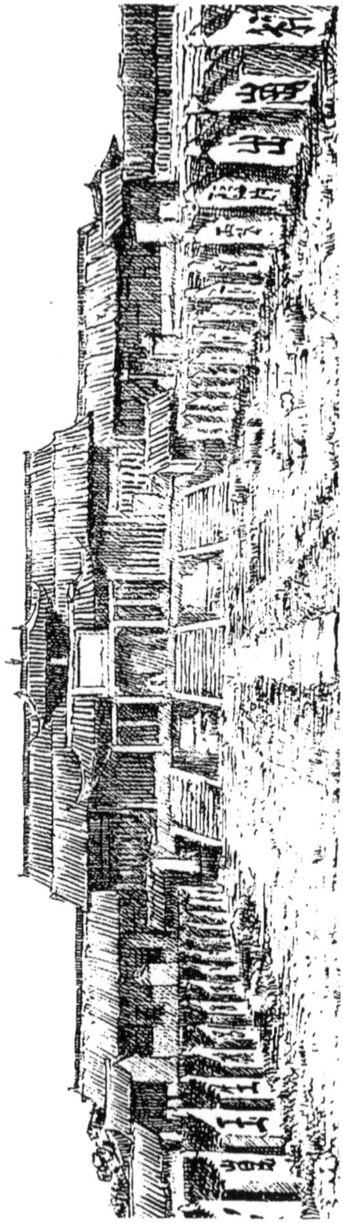

necessary examinations. There are six examinations possible.

The first examination is held yearly by the district magistrate; it lasts for three days, and the candidate has to write two essays, one on poetry. The second examination is held (generally a few months later) in a prefectural town, and is therefore called Fu Kau, or country examination. The students who pass this examination are called Shu Tsai. The third examination (only open to those who have passed the previous one) is the triennial one, which takes place in the capital of each province, as above described, and is called the Ju Jen degree. This time the candidate has to write several more essays than for the Shu Tsai degree; the quality most valued in these essays is skill in quotation, both as to the number of quotations made from the classics and the way in which they are combined—this might aptly be compared to a string of pearls. The candidates who obtain the Ju Jen degree are alone eligible for the degree of Tsin Sze. This fourth examination takes place triennially at Peking. The candidate is confined for nine days in a small compartment in the examination building. No matter how great the discomfort of this confinement may be, he has to write nine essays. I obtained the most fascinating little crib containing the whole classics, not larger than one inch square, which would offer a severe temptation under such circumstances to the most conscientious student! If the candidate is successful with his nine essays he receives the title of Tsin Sze, but if not, he may be appointed to a clerkship of a more or less important nature, according to the merit of his essays.

A yet higher degree may be obtained called the Tien Sze, because it is held in one of the buildings of the Imperial Palace. The student at the head of the list is called Cheong Yuan; the second is Paun Yien; the third is called Tua Hwa, and the fourth Chuan Lo To. Their official title, which is also given to other successful candidates in this examination, is Han Lin Yuan Shu Chi Sze, and they are obliged to study for the next three years at the Han Lin Yuan for the next examination. The successful candidates are retained at the Han Lin, and the unsuccessful ones receive posts of lesser importance, such as magistracies and other civil appointments. They are considered to have a first claim to all such appointments.[1]

This old examination system is being replaced by one in which Western subjects are to a large extent taking the place of the classics. Since 1904 the degrees of the Ju Jen and Han Lin have been granted in this way to students educated abroad and examined on their return to China. At the present time there are about 300 Chinese students in England, studying mainly law, medicine, engineering, and manufactures: some are still in public schools, grammar schools, &c.; others are at the English or Scotch universities.

In the accompanying sketch of a scholar, the gold

[1] For these details I am indebted to the courtesy of Mr. Ivan Chen, of the Imperial Chinese Legation.

1. SCHOLAR

2. SOUTHERN SERVANT

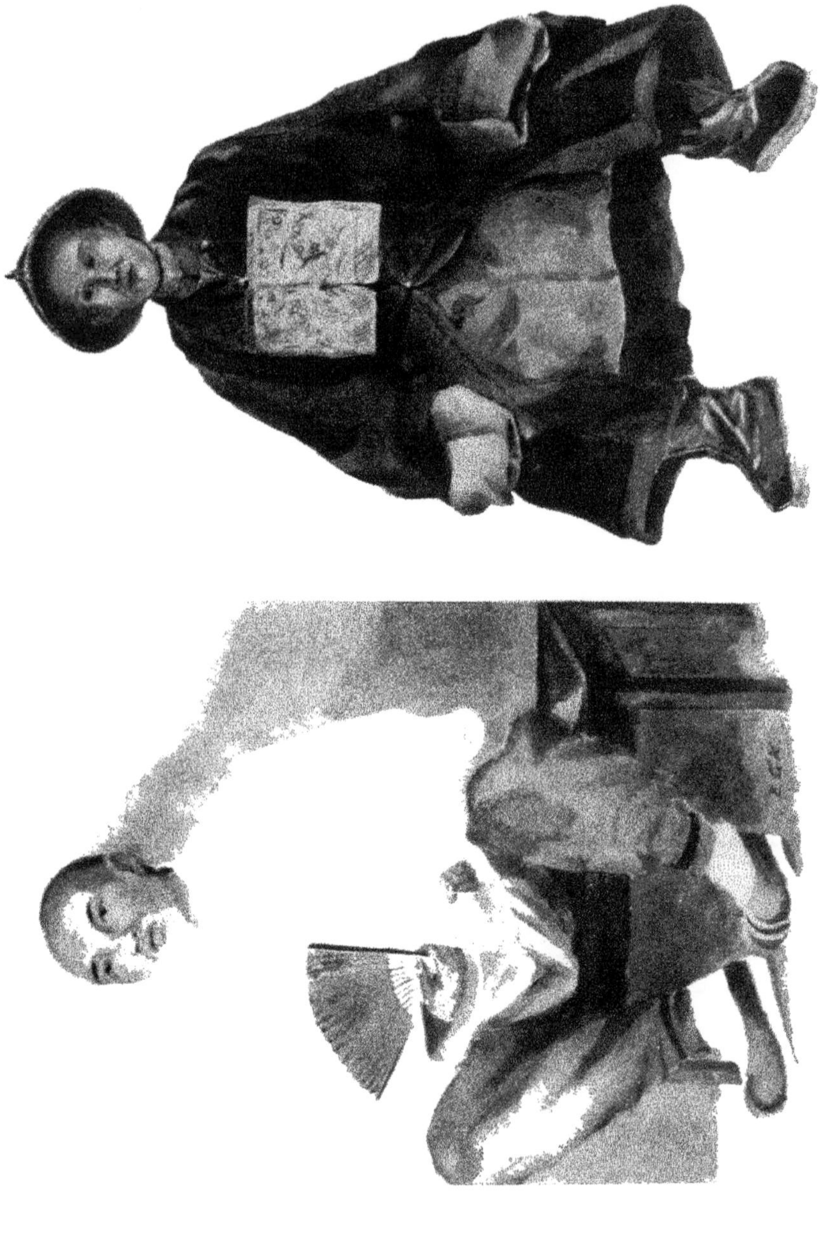

square worn on the chest and a corresponding one on the back are equivalent to the hoods granted by our universities, and the different designs on them indicate the kind of degree. Wives of scholars have also the right to wear the same insignia as their husbands.

The city of Taiyüanfu as described in this chapter is already a thing of the past. Now a railway comes to its very gates. New European-looking buildings are springing up in every direction ; the streets are being widened and properly paved, officials drive about in smart broughams, and there is a daily delivery of letters instead of a private post once a fortnight.

I return to Tientsin and take up the thread of my narrative in 1907. No sooner had we arrived there than a Chinese friend, clad in a beautiful maize-coloured silk gown, came to call. He had come from Peking expressly to meet us, and escorted us there next day, being an old friend of my Taiyüanfu days. We were seen off in the *Chinese* railway (so much preferable to the German and Belgian lines) next day by one of the directors, who had kindly ordered a special reserved carriage for us. A few hours of pleasant travel, with tea served on board, brought us to the special goal of our ambition—Peking.

CHAPTER XI

Peking

WE reached Peking after dark, which was fortunate, as the glamour of all one's youthful dreams was not at once dispelled by being brought face to face with the prosaic European Legations which lie just within the gates. At the railway station, which is close to the great gate leading to the Summer Palace, we emerged into a shouting, jostling Chinese crowd, and were put into rickshas by the friends—Chinese and American—who had come to meet us. Police were keeping order after a fashion most necessary, for I saw a pushing fellow seize an unlucky man who was having a dispute and fling his ricksha to the ground as if it were a dirty rag. When we and our luggage had been safely packed into a ricksha we were swiftly drawn over the most shocking roads, through the great gloomy gates, into the city. Everywhere we seemed surrounded by towering walls of vast thickness. Over the chief gateway is a large temple containing the tutelary deities, which may give some idea of this thickness. It rises tier above tier and is painted a beautiful Venetian red, and the tiles are a bright blue-green ; the overhang-

CITY WALL OF PEKING

CITY WALL OF PEKING

ing eaves are of carved woodwork, painted blue and green and gold. Opposite this entrance is that of the imperial palace, above which one sees its orange-coloured tiles. From the top of the wall one gets a fine view of the long approach to the palace, gateway beyond gateway, in true Chinese style, and stretching on every side an endless vista of trees and roofs of the city. Formerly this was a favourite *point de vue* for watching royalties when they drove out, but now no one is allowed to do this, and notice is sent to the various embassies requesting foreigners to stay indoors when the royal family is taking an airing!

From the great gate eastward, part of the wall was held during the siege by the Americans, aided by twenty British and twenty Russian soldiers. One morning they awoke to find that during the night the Chinese had built a tower on it, of about twenty feet high, overlooking them. All the next day they had to lie close under their criss-cross defences, but it was clear that unless the tower were seized the Chinese would soon be masters of the situation. Captain Myers planned its capture, inviting volunteers to help him, and naturally the twenty British soldiers responded promptly. It was arranged that the Americans and British should get round it from the outer side of the wall, and the Russians join them from the inner side. When the time came for the plan to be carried out it was quite successful, except for the fact that no Russians took part in it, and that Captain Myers was severely wounded. As we stood listening to the story from one of the besieged we saw a touching scene in the American barracks below us. A man entered carrying home mails, and shouted out the fact. In a moment men came flying from every quarter of the hitherto empty yard with hands outstretched ; one could almost see the throb of delight with which the letters were seized. But this was in time of peace, and we could but dimly realise what far greater excitement was caused by the arrival of a messenger from Tientsin during the siege, after the sickening suspense of hope deferred. How deadly must have been the disappointment when the brief message ran that help was coming, but not a word as to *when*, merely the egoistic remark that in Tientsin they also had been besieged !

My sketch is taken on the top of the wall, and shows the part held by the Americans : it extends from the spot where I was standing as far as the building over the great gate, and the embassies are close below the wall on the right-hand side.

The accounts of the siege which we heard from all those who had lived through it agreed in one respect—the singular defencelessness of the besieged, and the ease with which they might have been wiped out—leading one to conceive the probability of what a Chinese resident told me, that their commander-in-chief determined that this should not be done. The time that followed the siege seems to have been really in many ways worse than the siege itself for those who remained in Peking.

Far the most impressive monument here is the altar of Heaven, which lies at a short distance outside the inner city in an ancient park, surrounded by a high wall. Passing through a simple doorway, you drive in your ricksha up an avenue of acacias for a short distance till you come to another wall, and here you must get out before entering the inner park. The trees were already beginning to look autumnal (November) as we made our way across the coarse grass into another high-walled enclosure, surrounded by a moat; we had to knock for admittance to a large courtyard, where the Emperor spends the night once a year before offering the great national sacrifice to Heaven. All the roofs of the buildings round the courtyard were of brilliant green tiles, and contrasted beautifully with the marble terrace, balustrades, and bridges. From here the Emperor goes at 5.30 A.M., accompanied by his courtiers, to the great marble altar of Heaven, about one-fifth of a mile distant across the park. Fine stone pylons lead to the altar, but the paths are overgrown with grass, and there is a look of desolation brooding over the place. The altar is a high circular platform of marble, with three short flights of steps leading up from each of the four points of the compass. The Emperor ascends these steps, accompanied by his courtiers, but only those over seventy years of age may go up the top flight and remain with him while he kneels in the centre, under the vault of Heaven, to offer his sacrificial prayer. No spectator is ever allowed to be present. At the foot of the steps the sacrifice is offered, but the Emperor is no longer obliged to slay the bullock himself, as in the old days. This act is delegated to a high official. The sacrificial beasts are reared and kept in the surrounding park. Twelve bales of cloth are burnt in great braziers as an offering to Heaven; they are placed at short distances from one another, and each time there is a new emperor a new brazier is erected. Everything is round, as being emblematic of Heaven, while in the temple to Earth everything is square, because the earth is supposed to be square, and in the latter the sacrifices are buried instead of being burnt, so that they may go down instead of up!

Close to the altar of Heaven is a small round enclosure containing a temple roofed with gorgeous lapis-lazuli blue tiles, like the adjoining temple of Heaven, which is erected on a marble platform exactly similar to the altar of Heaven.

There are two particularly fine Buddhist temples at Peking, one outside and the other inside the walls, the former being a monastic establishment and swarming with degraded-looking monks. It has the imperial double-storied roofs of a noble orange colour, and it was a picturesque sight to see the orange-robed monks trooping into the courtyard to evening prayer. There were many young boys amongst them, probably sent from Manchuria as a thank-offering for the recovery of a father from severe illness, and consequently doomed to a life of idleness and ignorance. The Buddhist monks are notorious in this city for their low

TEMPLE OF HEAVEN

cted on a marb

morals, and the signs of it are unmistakably stamped upon their faces; they do no work of any kind, and live upon the alms given by worshippers or which they have begged, according to the rules of the order. It is comic to see the Buddhist monks strutting along under huge orange umbrellas, nose in air, followed by a servant carrying the compulsory begging bowl! The head of the monastery is an incarnate Buddha. In the chief temple of this monastery is a gigantic standing figure of Buddha, and you can go up a staircase to inspect the head, which is otherwise hardly visible in the gloom of the lofty building, whose only light comes from the doorway. In the smaller buildings are other Buddhas of various kinds, and the Bodhisatwa, the 1000-handed goddess Kwanyin.

In the Lama temple, three miles outside the city, there are figures of the goddess of mercy, beside the three seated Buddhas, and she is to be found in many of the temples. She was originally a man, but had the heart of a woman! Here we were dreadfully pestered by dirty children, whom the priest tried ineffectually to keep in order. Each courtyard we came to had to be unlocked, but he always let them pass through with us, clamouring for money. The great feature of the yellow temple is a marble monument to the memory of a lama who came from Tibet and died of smallpox. It is composed of white marble, and the centre has a fine series of carvings round it illustrating scenes from the life of the Buddha. Unfortunately, after the siege of Peking French soldiers were quartered here, and they are said to have amused themselves by knocking off the head of every single figure. The effect of the white marble and gold in the midst of hoary cypresses is very fine. This is where the Dalai Lama was lodged during his stay in Peking.[1] It must have been a picturesque scene on his arrival, when he entered the sacred precincts, passing between two long rows of yellow-clad monks. Would that we had been there to see it, instead of at such a dreary season! We had come in the face of considerable difficulties, but it was well worth while; the wind blowing when we started in rickshas soon developed into a typical Chili dust-storm, and soon after leaving the city the men declared they could go no further. Having no other chance of visiting the place, we determined not to be baulked and set out on foot. We struggled bravely forward through stinging, blinding dust till we got under the lee of its high wall. The return journey was not so bad, as the wind was behind us, and we could enjoy watching other passengers whom we met in the city lying as flat as they could in rickshas, and with handkerchiefs spread over their faces. We were almost unrecognisable when we got in, and it was a well-nigh hopeless task to get rid of the dust from hair and clothes.

For once a Chinese cart seemed a desirable thing, and we were glad to find one waiting to take us to a

[1] The late Dowager Empress conferred on him the title of "Sincere and loyal Spreader of Civilization," in addition to his old title of "The great, righteous, and complacent Buddha of Western Heavens."

Chinese friend's house, where we were to spend the remainder of our time at Peking. The streets are broad and fairly well policed, but their roughness is extraordinary, and when you sit cross-legged in the place of honour at the back of a springless cart you are tossed from side to side like a ball, and your head bumped unmercifully, till you have learned how to avoid it. You get much more exercise than if you walk; the only compensation is that you know you are doing the correct thing. Our host, who is a successful young doctor, explained that he was obliged to go in a cart to visit high-class patients, instead of on his bicycle, though it took up a great deal more time.

We were glad to have a Chinaman to take us shopping, for our mouths watered to see the attractive things in the native shops. The minute that a European enters, up go the prices to at least double, if not treble; so we had an amusing but not very successful time in them. Our kind host could not bear to see us being cheated, and it was with the utmost difficulty that I persuaded him to get me a black spotted leopard-skin coat lined with lovely blue silk, on which I had set my heart, as the shopman refused to come down to what he considered a reasonable price. He begged us to let him in future get what we wanted and have the things brought to his house for inspection: the main difficulty lay in the fact that we did not know what we wanted, for the most part; but about one thing I had no doubt, and that was specimens of the noted nail paintings. There was only one celebrated artist, and he was about to retire to his native province of Szchuan, but by great good luck we secured a book containing nine paintings done with the finger-nail, and two white silk scrolls. The designs are excellent, and it is difficult to see any difference from that of a brush in execution. The book is bound in Chinese style, simply between two wooden boards, with a plain band of gold running down one side for about three-quarters of its length, but no title on it.

A comparison between Chinese and Japanese art shows plainly their close connection, and if the Japanese excel in certain qualities, they have not the virility which characterises the Chinese, from whom all their art is derived. It was towards the close of the fourth century A.D. that a systematic criticism of art and a history of painters was begun in China. The canons of pictorial art were laid down, and it will help us to understand and appreciate Chinese art better if we remember that the first and most important of their six canons is "the Life movement of the Spirit through the Rhythm of Things." Though their art is mainly decorative, it possesses marvellous vitality and poetic imagination. At the Chinese Court there were fifteen artists in attendance, ready to depict anything that the Dowager Empress might wish to have painted.

A distinguished lady, closely allied to the Empress, kindly gave me a sitting one morning ; but as she was at the time exempted from attendance at Court on account of ill-health, she was unable to wear full dress—namely, the large Manchu coiffure—which is so heavy

1. A LADY OF QUALITY

2 AN OFFICIAL

... he was about to retire to his native

a.

... one with the finger-

... silk scrolls. The designs are

... is difficult to see any difference from

... execution. The book is bound in

... wooden boards,

... runs down one side for

...ters of its length ... title on it.

... between Chinese and Japanese art

... their close ... and if the

... a certain ... were not the

... characterises the Chinese, from whom

... derived. ... close of

... A.D. ... of

... in China. The

... will help

... better if

... important of their

... of the spirit through

... is mainly

... poetic

... fifteen

... ready to depart ... that the

... might wish to have painted.

... Empress,

... s she was

... Court on ac-

... the ... to wear full dress—

... which is so heavy

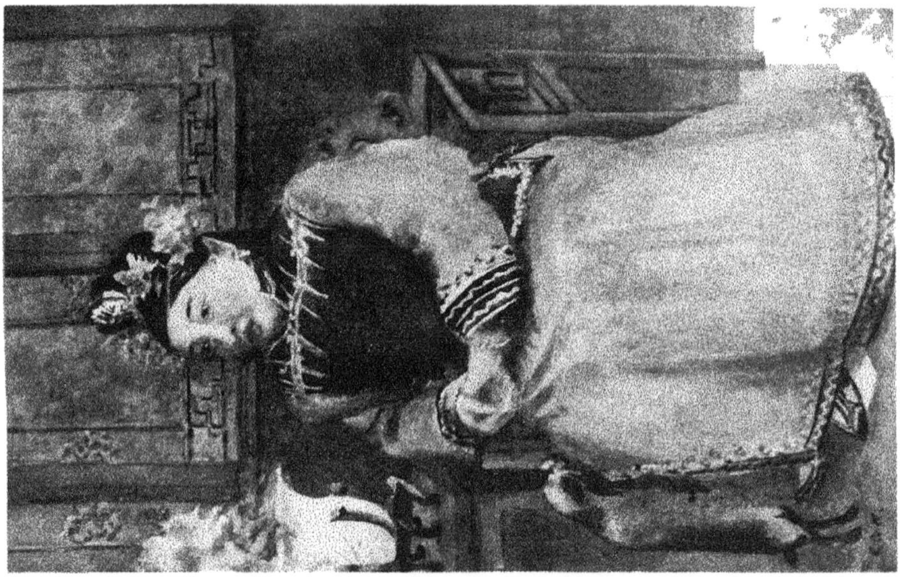

that the Empress decided to allow it to be replaced by large black satin bows. It is difficult to fasten the framework securely to the head, over which the hair is arranged, so the coiffure is usually made with false hair, and it is funny to see withered old hags in the streets wearing these, with a large flower stuck jauntily at the side. I found my sitter a very difficult one to paint, as she was heavily painted (in a different sense), and the square scarlet under-lip and absence of line in the upper eyelid gave a wooden expression to the whole face, which was unusually large, and surmounted by a perfect flower-bed. It would have been easier to express the dignity of her carriage had she been standing, but although she offered to do so, I felt it was impossible to take advantage of her good-nature when I knew she was ill. Her hands were slender and beautifully shaped, but she wore no rings; her feet were very small and shod in artistically embroidered Manchu shoes with white soles—nearly two inches thick (the Manchus never bind their feet). Unfortunately, the handsome heliotrope gown and short jacket were trimmed with European braid, and owing to the cold weather they were wadded, which lends a clumsy appearance to the whole figure. Her charming little black pug belongs to the celebrated palace breed.

It was not till after we had enjoyed tea and cakes that I was allowed to begin the portrait; and the prince came in to make our acquaintance, so that a good deal of time was taken up, and I was only able to make a hasty sketch, to be finished later on. Then the lady said we must certainly be hungry and insisted on our stopping to dinner, saying she herself was very hungry—how much more so must we be, who had worked while she did nothing. My friend protested that she had done nothing at all, being reduced to silence by her ignorance of the language, to which came the charming retort, "You will be fatigued, then, by your good intentions!" All our protests as to other engagements were overruled, and we sat down, at the other end of the room from where we had been sitting before, to a sumptuous repast, consisting of every kind of meat and vegetable, served in small pieces in innumerable little dishes. In the centre of the table there was a charming set of nine dishes, which are generally used for sweetmeats, but which our hostess had thought would be equally nice for meat—an innovation we thoroughly appreciated, as they looked so much prettier than separate ones. From these dishes we were continually helped to cold chicken, duck, sausage, pigeons, eggs, ham, and other less recognisable dainties. Round these were more dishes of hot vegetables, pickled meat and vegetable, rissoles, fried meat balls, stewed meat, cabbage and meat, &c., &c., from all of which our hostess continued to serve us with her own chop-sticks, eating but little herself, according to the Chinese etiquette. We were given spoons and forks, as she shrewdly suspected our inability to wield chop-sticks. Little bowls of rice were also handed round, and as soon as we stopped eating she did the same. Next came bowls of soup, each containing two eggs, and this concluded the solid part of the feast; as soon as we had retired to the other end of the room tea was brought, with preserved crab-apples, apple jam, and pea-nuts. Part of the dinner, we were told, was prepared by men and part by women cooks.

Before we took leave the children came in to be introduced. All the young people are learning English, and shook hands in English style—namely, with *us*, instead of with *themselves*. Many polite questions were asked as to our families, our clothes, and the price of the Viennese gown I was wearing, and my amethyst pendant. Silk is considered the only material for a handsome dress in China, and precious stones are practically unknown, jade being the only one worn.

Finally we made our adieux, accompanied to the outermost courtyard by our kind hostess; and the next day she sent me a fascinating assortment of Chinese paints, each done up separately in the neatest little parcel, containing either a bottle or a little box. We came away much impressed by the indescribable charm of Chinese manners, and many a time afterwards I felt how *gauche* we were in comparison. We drove away in our cart for politeness' sake, but a short ride in it after such a feast would have had disastrous consequences, so we quickly transferred ourselves to rickshas as soon as we were out of sight of the palace.

It would be wearisome to the reader to describe all the interesting places we saw in Peking, but there is still one that I must mention—the Hall of the Classics. It is the centre of the great examination system of the past, and probably will never again have its old importance. Here the final examination took place of all the students, from every part of the vast Empire, who had succeeded in passing all other examinations. The Emperor himself presided, and received the homage of successful candidates, seated upon a handsome carved throne. Round the walls of the great court are tablets on which are inscribed the whole of the classics. The old examination system has been abolished, and already at Peking the very building where the provincial examinations were held has been destroyed.

Before leaving Peking our host introduced us to the friend whom he had found to act as our interpreter during our long journey from north-east to south-west of the Empire. Mr. Ku was a young man of official family, who had been trained at St. John's College, Shanghai, and spoke English well. He was essentially a scholar, of gentle and amiable manners, honourable and guileless. During our five months together we never found him lacking in tact or discretion, and we were able without hesitation to place our affairs entirely in his hands. Fortunate is the traveller who likes his companions better at the end of such a journey than at the beginning !

Mr. Ku's father had a narrow escape for his life,

1. BOXER

KACHIN WOMAN

some to the reader to describ
aces we saw in Pek
must mention—the
centre of the g
and probably will hav
Here the final ex tool
udents, from every
ad succeeded in othe
The Emperor an
nage of successful
ne wall
urt are tablets on scribe
the classics. ratio
abolished, and
where the provinc
destroyed.
Peking our

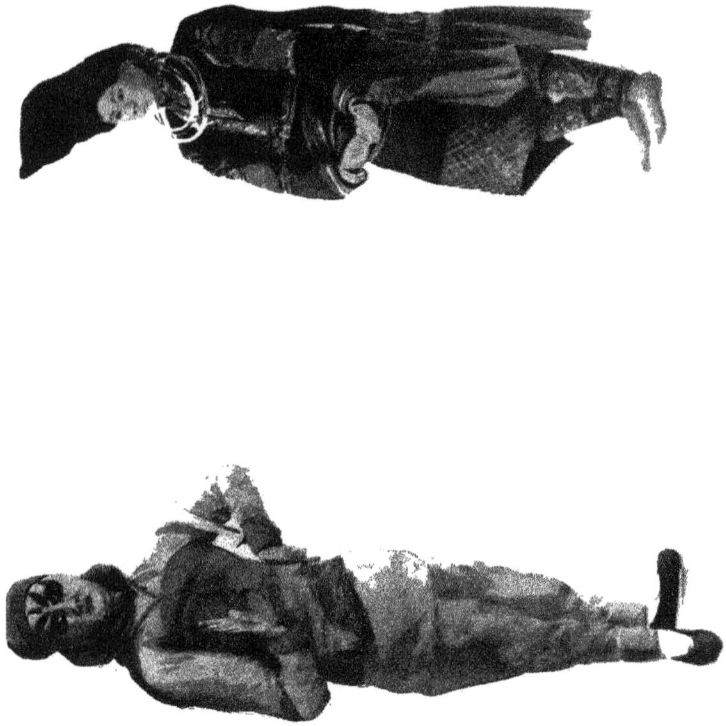

like many other Chinese officials, during the troubles of 1900. He was seized one day by Boxers, who prepared to kill him: when he asked why they were doing this they said it was because he was a Christian. He assured them he was not, but they refused to believe it, and it was only after repeated remonstrances that they said they would put it to the proof. This was done by means of lighting a piece of paper: if it burnt away entirely, the Boxers said that would show he was not a Christian, but if it didn't, then he should be put to death. Happily the paper was dry and burnt up, but the Boxers, although they spared life in this case, demanded a heavy sum of money and a quantity of rice. Although the Boxers began by being patriotic fanatics, they soon turned into mere plunderers. The sketch gives the costume of a Peking Boxer, with upraised hand making a military sign; but they had no regular uniform, and merely wore red as a distinctive mark.

We only spent six days at Peking, as we felt we must hurry on, much as we should have liked to spend weeks there instead of days.

CHAPTER XII

The Péhan Railway: from Peking to Hankow

THIS line extends a distance of 700 English miles from Peking to Hankow. The railway was constructed by a Belgian syndicate, but it is really a combination of French, Belgian, and Russian interests, which were successful in outbidding American proposals. The Belgians proved themselves more successful diplomatists than the Americans, and struck a bargain with the Chinese, in 1897, of such a nature that it had to be completely altered afterwards. The arrangement certainly does not bear a creditable aspect. Indeed, the whole history of railway enterprise in China makes sorry reading. British protests were ignored, and a working agreement was made, giving the Belgian syndicate full rights over the line for forty years. In the prospectus which they issued they professed to have obtained the right to carry the railway through from Hankow to Canton, but events have conclusively proved that, although they attempted to obtain this right, it was refused. An American combination won the concession in 1898, but it was cancelled in 1905—little progress having been made—and it is to

MR. KU

CHAPTER XII

han Railway: fr
to Hankow

S line extends a distance
les from Peking to Hankow
constructed by a Belgian
mbination of French, Belg
ich were successful in outb
The Belgians proved the
omatists than the Ameri
h the Chinese, in 1897.
to be completely altered
t certainly does not bear
whole history of railway
r reading. British pr
ng agreement was made, gr
all rights over the line for
ctus which they issued th
ed the right to carry the
ow to Canton, but events ha
t, although they attempted

be a Chinese line from Hankow to Canton. An English engineer had already strongly advocated the value of such a line, and the Chinese are made to realise more clearly every day the advisability or keeping the railways as far as possible in their own hands.

One of the most striking drawbacks of the Péhan railway is that no goods can safely be sent by it. Our luggage was fortunately so small that we had it all in the carriage with us—two suit-cases, two bed-bags, and a hold-all being all that we allowed ourselves for the journey through the interior. We had sent our other luggage round from Shanghai to Burma, so that we might travel as lightly as possible. During the whole of our journey we never lost a single article, and it was a disheartening consideration that it was only when we came in contact with Europeans that we had any need for care.

Together with the right to build the Péhan line, the Belgian syndicate obtained a mining concession of great value at Lincheng in the province of Chili. So much with regard to the Chinese railways.

We started in the grey dawn to take the 7 A.M. train to Hankow, and as the only weekly express started the wrong day for us, we decided to go by the ordinary mail. According to continental custom, there is a considerable difference in price between the two, and we paid the same price for first-class ordinary tickets as we should have done for second-class by the express. The carriages are not so good, but we found them comfortable, and infinitely cleaner than on the German line. In fact, a man came round periodically with a feather brush to dust us out, and this was sadly needed across the dusty plains of Chili and Honan, which it took us two days to traverse. The carriages are broad, and we had one to ourselves, next door to a handy little kitchen. Perhaps it was with this fact in view that mine host's cook brought us two live chickens, tied by a string, as provision for the journey! But we had started in such excellent time that the doctor sent him off from the station post-haste to get cooked ones instead, and he returned triumphant with two well-spiced creatures packed in a basket, covered with leaves. We were only dependent, therefore, on the kitchen for hot water, and it was a great boon to have as much as we wanted both for drinking and washing. Our servant Liu—who had been found for us and partially trained by the doctor—was allowed to come along and wash up for us and do any odd jobs we might want.

The train only runs during the day, but we got permission to stay in it at night, and having bedding with us, we were able to be quite comfortable. It was much less fatiguing than having to turn out and go to an inn, especially as we started again at 6 A.M. The vast plains that we passed through looked very deserted, as the harvest is practically over: the persimmon trees were nearly bare of fruit, but the Indian corn still made vivid patches of colour on the threshing-floors, and occasionally we saw monkey-nuts being sifted from

THE BRAKEMAN ON THE PÉHAN RAILWAY

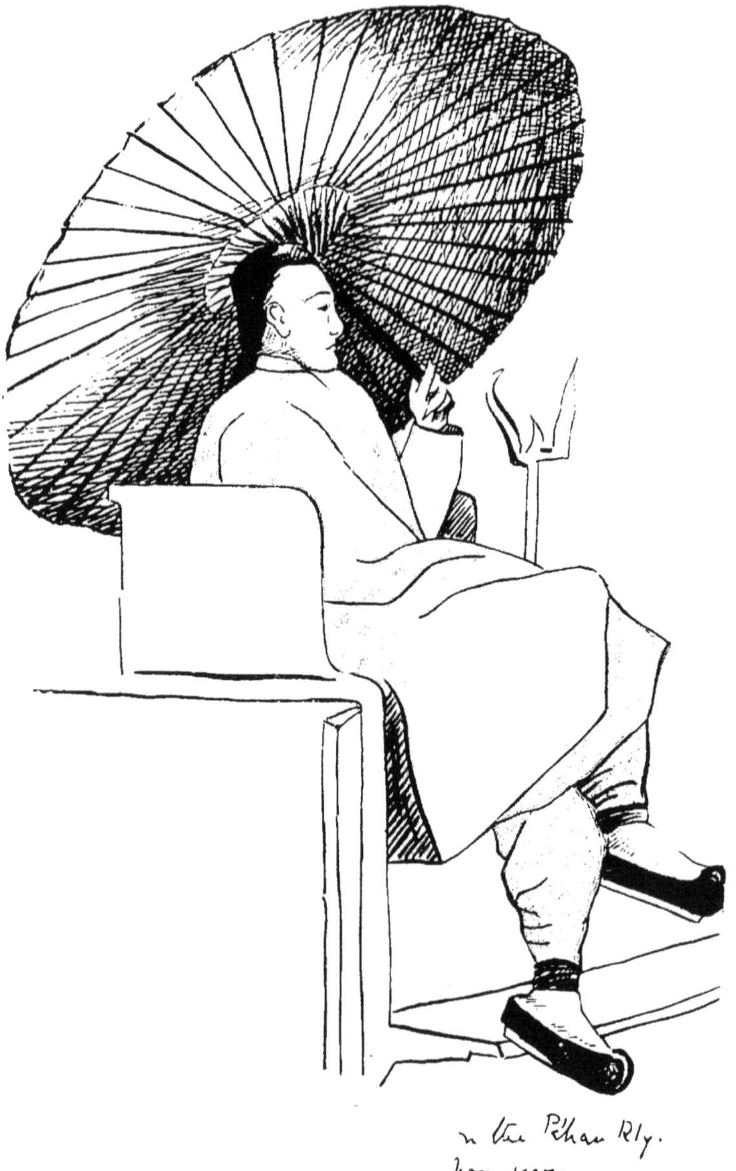

on the Pehan Rly.
Nov 1907.

the sandy soil, which is particularly adapted to their culture.

We found the stations on the Péhan railway more varied and amusing than those in Shantung ; we could really have supplied all our needs in the way of food at them, as there were excellent bread, chickens, eggs, various kinds of fruit, and many Chinese delicacies to be had ; but naturally we preferred carrying our own supplies.

On the second day we came to the most interesting point in the journey—the crossing of the Hwang Ho (Yellow River). It is a single-line bridge, nearly two miles long, and looks far too fragile to withstand the swirl of the waters when the river is full. It is a screw-pile erection, and was extremely difficult and costly to build, owing to the shifting sands and depth of mud.

The choice of a spot for a bridge has been criticised somewhat severely on account of changes in the course of the river, but its nine changes during 2000 years make an engineer study the matter with very great care, and one must hope that the right spot has been chosen. The bed of the river is simply a quicksand, and it proved extremely difficult to reach any solid foundation. The rock and stone at first used to strengthen the foundations was simply swallowed by the quicksand, and it was necessary to make a foundation of what can only be described as matting, made by twisting together the branches of trees, on which tons of stones were piled round the screw-piles, and these were again protected from the down-flowing tide by triangular arrangements of wooden piles. The screw-piles are placed in sets of four, six, eight, and ten, and joined together by powerful stanchions and girders, and they reach a depth of some forty-four feet. The train crawled across the bridge in a most gingerly way, and one would certainly hesitate to risk crossing it at flood-tide. As one looked down on the water (more like chocolate cream than anything else) eddying round the supports, there was an evil fascination about it. An Indian engineer explained to us that the Chinese method of damming the river is exactly the opposite to ours—namely, they darn it *below* the bridge, and we *above*. It was a relief to get safely across its interminable length: the time went so slowly that one might almost forget the notice-board at one end, saying, "Fleuve jaune, rive nord," before reaching the one at the other end, "Fleuve jaune, rive sud." At this point in the journey we left the Great North China Plain extending to the farther side of Peking, came into more varied country, and approached the hills, which before we had only seen at intervals looming in the distance. The railway goes through a tunnel, the first to be made in China, and emerges into the Yangtze valley.

On the third day the scenery we passed through was beautiful, and we came to quite a different vegetation. The Scotch firs on the steep loess hillsides reminded us pleasantly of home, and even a view of the Great Wall at one point did not altogether dispel the

GREAT WALL

illusion. Why the Great Wall extends down here it would be hard to say, for it could scarcely be of much use in its shrunken dimensions to keep out invaders. The Great Wall was erected along the northern frontier of China for a distance of about 1500 miles, in the year 214 B.C., by Chin Hwang Tu. The amount of material required to build it is said to be seventy times as much as that required for building the largest of the pyramids. The part of the wall we saw was a spur running down from the Great Wall between the provinces of Shansi and Chili; there are other similar spurs from the Great Wall. At the foot of the hill are rice-fields.

As we came farther south the vegetation changed. Instead of cornfields we saw rice-fields, mostly under water; and more and more the water increased in volume, till we found ourselves skirting large lagoons, with countless little boats on their surface, and large fishing-nets, which brought up a shining harvest of little fish. Many huts are built on land which must frequently be submerged, as is the case along the Yangtze valley.

Sometimes we saw beds of bamboos, for which the climate is too cold farther north. Water buffaloes replaced the other cattle, for the obvious reason that they are much better suited to work in swampy grounds.

At sunset we reached Hankow (so called because it is on the Han river), and were kept waiting a long time at the first station, close to the banks of the Yangtzekiang, so that it was dark by the time we reached the town. We drew up alongside a crowd of people, dimly illumined by the gay Chinese lanterns they were carrying, and found it difficult to distinguish the friends who had come to meet us. Nearly every one carries a lantern, or has a servant to do it, for the place is miserably lighted. The station is in the middle of the foreign concession, and you might easily imagine yourself in a poorly lighted London suburb, as you pass big warehouses and shops and suburban villas. It is the centre of the commercial life of the place, and there is a large European population.

All along the river-bank the city stretches for miles, and across the river is the town of Wuchang, to which ferries ply continually. If the wind is against you it may take an hour or more to get across, and you could easily imagine yourself on the sea. Indeed, it is nothing uncommon to go across in calm weather to pay a call, and for the wind to rise suddenly and prevent your coming back for a couple of days. At Wuchang there are various missions with hospitals and schools. At one of these we saw a slave girl who had been almost burnt to death with incense sticks by an enraged mistress, and then bricked up in a wall to die of starvation. She will probably never entirely recover the shock to the system. Large boat-loads of girls are continually passing down the river from the province of Szechwan, we were told, for sale at the ports; and although there has recently been an edict prohibiting the traffic, that edict is a dead letter.

Many slave girls are not badly treated, but in fits of passion a Chinese mistress becomes capable of diabolical cruelty. One child was brought to the hospital at Taiyūan Fu, some years ago when I was there, almost dead. She had been beaten and knocked about and bitten till she was one mass of bruises and sores, and was almost blind and quite lame. She screamed at first if any one came near her, and it was plain that kindness was a thing unknown. Soon she learnt that she had come into a new world, and responded beautifully to the new treatment. Her face lighted up with joy at any small gift, a flower or a sweet, and the necessary suffering caused by dressing her wounds was borne in heroic silence. Her one dread was lest she should recover so as to have to return to her old mistress. Several months of diplomatic negotiations passed before her mistress was persuaded to make her over as a gift to the hospital, on account of her incurable lameness and blindness, which rendered her practically useless.

So much has been said about the cruelty of the Chinese as a race, that I cannot forbear pointing out one or two things that have struck me. The Chinaman never appears to be cruel from innate love of cruelty for its own sake of sport, and I have never seen or heard in China of the atrocities which make travelling in southern Italy and Spain a misery to any one who loves animals. Cruelty for the love of money—such as that witnessed on the Congo and elsewhere—is not to be found in China, except in isolated cases, such as in the gaols. If it were not for the humanising influences of Christianity, I believe that we should be a more brutal race than the Chinese, for unhappily the sporting instinct, which we so strongly possess, is closely allied to cruelty. A Chinaman looking on at many a football match in Lancashire or Yorkshire might reasonably have much to say on the subject of kicking, for instance, as a proof of our brutality. Another point that is apt to be overlooked is that the Chinese are extraordinarily insensitive to pain; witness every operating theatre in the country, where anæsthetics are much less used or required than for Europeans. There is no denying that the Chinese can be unspeakably cruel when under the influence of passion, but not more so than Europeans; and that Chinese punishments are barbarous in the extreme; but there is little doubt they will soon be altered and brought into line with Western ideas, if one may judge from other changes now taking place.

There is a Bund at Hankow running along the river-side as at Shanghai, but it is not nearly so fine a one. Large ships pass daily between the two cities; for Hankow is a most flourishing place, the centre of the tea trade, and in its warehouses is packed all the tea for the Russian market which can be despatched to Russia without transhipment.[1] Immediately to the east of Hankow, and only separated from it by the

[1] Hankow is six hundred miles from the sea-coast, but ocean-going ships can come right up the river to that point, and smaller steamers go yet another four hundred miles to Ichang.

Han river, is the large town of Han-Yang, and this and Wu Chang form one big city with Hankow.

We had to wait a few days before we could get a steamer going to Ichang, and though small, we found it remarkably comfortable, so that we enjoyed our three days' trip. The country at first was flat, but there was always something to see—long, V-shaped flights of geese, or solid blocks of ducks. Herons, too, and many other kinds of birds we saw; and wild turkeys we *ate*, as well as pheasants.

The river was unusually high, but not too high, we ascertained, for us to get up the rapids. In consequence of the height of the river the tiny steam-launch had to be let down at one point, as well as continual soundings to be made to test the depth of the river-bed. This is always changing, especially during the fall of the river, and is one of the main difficulties of river navigation in China, making it most tiresome and dangerous.

Wet weather set in next day and lasted more or less for a week, so that the crags overhanging the banks near Ichang looked grand and forbidding as we steamed up to it.

CHAPTER XIII

On the Yangtze: Ichang to Wanhsien

WE reached Ichang on Sunday afternoon, and were glad to be in time for a service in the Presbyterian church, the last really home-like church we attended till we reached Burma. In all other churches there were things to remind us that we were in China, but here we were in Scotland once more, and this is the only station of the Scotch Established Church in China proper: they have a flourishing work, however, in Manchuria.

Ichang has quite a colony of Europeans. They were anxious to have a good road outside the town for the sake of exercise, and when we visited the tennis club we saw the one they had made. The whole surface of the ground for miles and miles is covered with mounds (=graves), so closely packed together that it is impossible to help treading on them if you leave the path. The Europeans knew there would be great difficulty in obtaining permission to make the road they wanted, so they subscribed the requisite funds among themselves and took French leave to make it. Before the Chinese had recovered from their

CHINESE GRAVES

on, and
in the
home-
In
nd us
tland
Scotch
have a

They
n for
tennis
whole
vered
together
f you
would
in obtaining permiss make the
they subscribed the requisite
revolver and took French leave to
the Chinese had recovered from their

Ichang
Nov 22.

surprise, or had decided what to do, the road was made. Then the Chinese acted in a truly magnanimous way. Instead of simply seizing it, as they had every right to do (according to my informant's story), they paid the Europeans all they had spent upon it, saying they must have the road in their own hands.

From my sketch some idea may be formed of the vast multitudes of graves outside Ichang: some have sticks planted in them with little paper streamers. Wherever we travelled we saw the same sight—endless graves speaking of the innumerable dead.

It took some time to make an agreement for a houseboat to take us from Ichang to Wanhsien, as the boatmen prefer to go as far as Chungking, where they can usually secure a fresh cargo for the return journey; but eventually the matter was satisfactorily settled. A nice clean boat was engaged, with three compartments and a good space for cooking at the back, above which a little god sat in a shrine. We decided to inhabit the two front rooms, and Mr. Ku and Liù the back one, and we hung up curtains to supplement the flimsy partitions, as they consisted of a few loose planks, with gaps of one or two inches wide between them, and at quite a slight touch they fell down.

It was a great convenience that our interpreter and our servant (who had also formerly been *his* servant) shared a room and always had their meals together. This is quite a usual arrangement in China, as there never seems to be any desire for privacy amongst the

Chinese, and servants are on a much more intimate footing with their masters than is the case with us.

The agreement for the boat was drawn up in writing, and the crew was to consist of nineteen men: the sum to be paid for the whole trip was 95 taels (about £14). As Hosie mentions in his book that he had to pay £45 for his boat to Chungking (about twice the distance, though the latter half is much the least arduous and dangerous), we were not dissatisfied with our bargain, although we were told we were paying quite too much.

The captain received 75 taels at starting, ten taels when half-way, and the remaining ten on arrival. Though the bargain was struck on Tuesday, we did not succeed in starting till Saturday morning, and in the mean time both we and the captain were busy with our preparations. We got wadded Chinese clothes, for it was beginning to get cold, and we thought (though in this we proved to be mistaken, for no curiosity was exhibited about us at any place we visited in European clothes) that they would save us from much inquisitive inspection in the western provinces. Long fur-lined silk coats we had got in Peking (about £3. 10s.), tall black velvet felt-lined boots (7s. 6d.), wadded silk jackets (7s. 6d.), black cloth (European) skirt, described on the bill in Mr. Chang's best English as "brewen fine cloth beetticoat" (£1. 2s. 6d.). Our heating and cooking apparatus had to be made—two impromptu charcoal stoves made out of packing-cases lined with bricks, a little oven to stand on the top, three pans with lids (made out of the ubiquitous kerosene tin), two tins, and a zinc kettle, all for the modest sum of 6s. 6d. As our servant's cooking capacity proved to be very limited—he proudly announced he could cook both a chicken and a pudding—we decided to trust rather to my experience, and we laid in a supply of stores, which are easily obtainable at Ichang.

The next point was to secure a red-boat (= lifeboat), for which we applied to the British Consul, and he again had to apply to the Chinese General, who is always willing to provide one gratis to foreign travellers. The Consul—like many of his class in China—at once suggested every possible difficulty, and seemed to think that at his request we should meekly turn round and go home again. He told us that he had just refused to give the bishop a passport for some ladies travelling into Szechwan, and we were thankful that we had got ours—though not without difficulty and vexation—elsewhere. As we were backed up by advice received at the British Embassy at Peking with regard to our journey, the Consul could not refuse to apply for the red-boat escort, though later in the day he had the satisfaction of telling us that none was available. Happily, however, one came in before we started, so that we had No. 48 assigned to us on Friday evening. It was very wet all day, but I found an interesting subject to paint in a family ancestral tablet. On the right-hand side is a drum for worship, and on the altar in front of the tablet is a bronze vase in which burning sticks of incense are placed. On certain days the members of the family prostrate themselves before it, and offerings of cakes and fruit are presented by them.

Ancestral worship dates from the earliest times, and has even to the present time the strongest hold upon people of all classes. The Emperor possesses seven shrines, representing his various ancestors; the nobles are allowed five shrines, and ordinary people have only one. The offerings are by no means costly or lavish, but at the same time they must not be mean; and it is related of a certain high official, with censure, that the sucking pig which he offered for his father was not large enough to fill the dish! Closely allied with ancestral worship is that greatest virtue of the Chinese, filial piety; and Confucius lays stress in his teaching on the spirit in which its duties are to be carried out, pointing out that it is best seen in endeavouring to realise the aims of the forefathers.

After dinner we made our way through the rain down the slippery bank to our boat, across a most shaky plank. The bare boards looked rather dull quarters for the night, and the wind whistled dismally, so our kind hosts offered to lend us deck-chairs and a good supply of newspapers to keep out draughts—an offer we thankfully accepted. Soon we had everything ship-shape, and began to accustom ourselves to the lullaby provided by nineteen snorers, packed like herrings into the few yards composing the forepart of the bcat.

We made a pretence of starting the next morning

ANCESTRAL TABLET

between seven and eight o'clock, heralded by a tremendous trampling overhead on our little roof, which must have been remarkably tough not to have given way. The mats used as an awning over the boatmen at night were stacked on our roof during the day. We slowly made our way by the aid of a sail for about half a mile up the river, alongside the town; then the men stopped for breakfast, and we were told that the captain had gone ashore to buy more bamboo towing-ropes. This took another hour or two. Again we started, but after another half-mile we drew up beside an island for a very long spell. *Festina lente* was evidently the watchword, and it took a great many exhortations through Mr. Ku, as interpreter, before we got the men started again. Eventually we succeeded in reaching the custom-house (ten miles up the river) by dusk, and there tied up for the night.

From that time we always started soon after daylight, and there was no lack of interest. The scenery became very grand—the banks were nearer to each other, and lofty crags rose precipitously from the riverside, often to a considerable height, 200 or 250 feet. Though the colour of the water is ugly and muddy, the vegetation is most beautiful, and the foliage of the azalea added greatly to the charm of the landscape. There was so little wind that the sail was practically useless, and the men shouted for the wind in vain. It is curious how much faith they have in shouting, despite their frequent failure. They were obliged to row, or go ashore and track. There is one long oar on each side of the boat, and it is worked by five or six men, who twist it to the accompaniment of a hoarse vocal noise—it can hardly be called a chant—and it sometimes rises to a veritable howl! Not infrequently one of the rowers stands on a plank on the outer side of the oar—namely, above the river—fixed at right angles to the boat. When the current is strong the men work in a sort of frenzy and stamp like elephants, their voices rising to a deafening din, assisted by those of the rest of the crew. Despite the cold they strip to the waist, and only put on their thin blue cotton coats when they go on shore to track.

One of the men, clad in a long coat, utilised an unwonted lull in his labours to wash his nether garment in the rice-tub which had just been emptied by the hungry men! His teeth were chattering with cold, and he shivered wofully in the raw air. The ten men who act as trackers and tow the boat are as nimble as cats and scale the rocks with marvellous rapidity, keeping up a rapid trot over the most uncompromising boulders, while two men follow them to clear the rope from obstructions. The ropes are made of bamboo, and look little qualified to stand the heavy strain of pulling the laden junks up the rapids. To these ropes the men are harnessed by short ropes, which they detach at pleasure. The trackers are often a quarter of a mile distant from the boat, for the river is very wide and winding in places, and frequently extra men have to be hired, augmenting their numbers up to

BLUE DAWN

one hundred or more for the worst rapids. Many a time a tracker has to dash into the swirling waters to free the rope, and his scanty clothing is flung off in the twinkling of an eye. Our red-boat was quite useful in taking the trackers on and off the shore, where the water was too shallow for us to go—and the red-boat men were friendly creatures, continually hovering round us night and day, ready for service. By means of little offerings of hot tea, &c., we soon got on the pleasantest terms, and often had little dumb-show conversations. These boats are very light, and have long narrow blue sails and blue-and-white striped awnings; the boat and military uniform are scarlet, so that they are readily distinguishable from all other craft on the river. Even their chopsticks are red: altogether they look extremely smart, and the boatmen are skilful and experienced men. Parcel-post boats have blue-and-white striped sails and a yellow sort of box in the centre of the boat to distinguish them. The letters do not go by water, but are carried by men overland.

There have been so many accidents on the river this season, owing to its fulness, that we determined to go ashore whenever we came to a rapid, and to take our luggage with us. We duly instructed the captain and also the red-boat men on the subject, but, to our surprise, on the third day we discovered that we had already come up one rapid, and before we knew it we were into a second. The fact is that the current is so strong, and the river altogether so tumultuous and vicious-looking, that to the uninitiated the rapids are not always different in appearance from the rest of the Yangtze, and most of the way through the gorges seems full of rapids. Getting round the sharp bends of the river is a difficult matter, and they frequently tie a rope from the boat round a boulder, while the trackers hold on to another fastened to the top of the mast, from which it can be lowered at will by means of a slip rope. The trackers strain every nerve, and frequently go on all-fours, and yet can't budge an inch. Sometimes they are obliged to let go, and then the junk slips back in the swirl of water, to the great danger of any others that may be in the rear.

The fourth day after leaving Ichang we had a very narrow escape of this sort. I had been admonishing the captain about his stupidity in following close behind a heavy large junk, and told him we ought to have been in front of it, by starting a little earlier in the morning. He was surly, and complained that it would have been necessary to get up so *very*, *very* early; but he was soon brought to repentance by something much more unpleasant than my words. We were waiting our turn to get round a sharp corner, and were moored to the bank, so we had no means of escape when the big junk suddenly swooped down upon us. A horrible grinding, tearing, crashing sound ensued, accompanied by violent yells from the men; but we gasped with relief to see our walls still intact, though our windows were shivered and the shutters torn off. The damage done was quite small,

YEH TAN RAPID

vicious-looking, that [illegible] are not always different [illegible] rest of the Yangtze, and [illegible] gorges seems full of rapids [illegible] bends of the river is a [illegible] frequently tie a rope from [illegible] while the trackers hold [illegible] of the mast, from which [illegible] means of a slip rope. [illegible] and frequently go on [illegible] an inch. Sometimes they [illegible] the junk slips back [illegible] great danger of any [illegible]

The fourth day [illegible] very narrow escape [illegible] hing the captain [illegible] close behind a heavy [illegible] ought to have been in [illegible] earlier in the morning. [illegible] that it would have been [illegible] very early, but he was [illegible] by something much [illegible] words. We were waiting [illegible] sharp corner and were [illegible] had no means of escape when [illegible] swooped down upon us. A [illegible] crashing sound [illegible] from the men, [illegible] walls still intact, though our windows [illegible] and the shutters torn off. The damage [illegible] quite small,

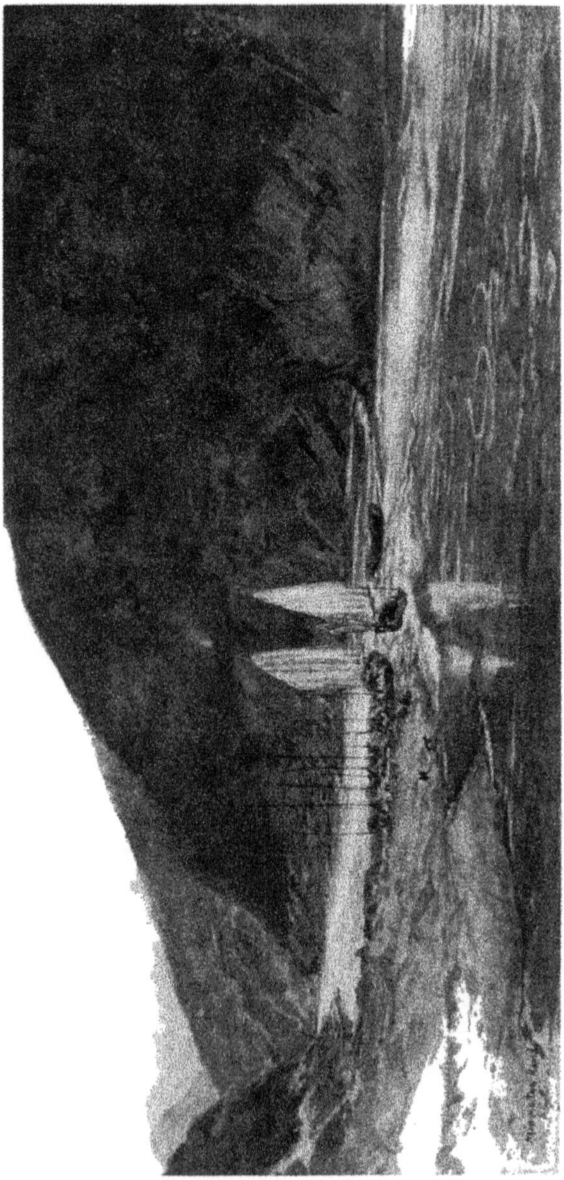

but it delayed us several hours that day, and caused us to be at the end of a long string of boats for getting up the big rapid next day.

The Yeh Tan rapid (nicknamed Mutton Point by the prosaic foreigner) is one of the most dangerous, and we made great preparations in case of accident, packing up our things carefully in oiled paper—a most useful Chinese article, as it is a very cheap kind of waterproof. Our men made quite other preparations, which they firmly believed in. A quantity of special sacred paper was waved—burning—over the front of the boat; incense sticks were fixed up and lighted; finally a cock was killed, and its blood and feathers plentifully bespattered around. This was extremely distracting to me, as I was well embarked on a sketch when it took place under my very eyes. The subject of the sketch was quite characteristic—a beautiful rosy russet hillside, with a temple peeping out of the trees, and a long narrow line of village above the high-water mark of the river. On the shingly river-bed were temporary booths used as restaurants.

Finding ourselves tied to the bank for an indefinite time, we began to cook our lunch; but no sooner was the pot boiling than our red-boat men appeared saying they had got up the rapid (they were not obliged to wait their turn like ordinary boats), and were come to escort us on shore. We asked if our boat was allowed to take precedence of the big junks, and were told that it was; and as our trackers had already gone ashore, it lent colour to the fiction, and we started off cheerfully enough. The boatmen shouldered our suit-cases, which we were afraid to risk, as they contained not only clothes and sketches, but money in the shape of lumps of silver called "tings," that were to last us for several weeks, and which weighed many pounds. It is really tiresome to have to carry money in this form and have it cut up and weighed in little bits, with which to buy the cash of the district, before you can purchase anything. In the more Europeanised East, Mexican dollars are used, also bank-notes; but from this time on we were obliged to use only the rough silver lumps and copper cash. Sometimes the reckoning was by taels and sometimes by dollars. The tael is an ounce of silver—namely, one and one-third English ounces—but there is no coin to represent the tael. The silver shoe is about fifty taels, but the taels vary in value at different places—the Peking tael is not the same, for instance, as the Hankow tael: altogether, the money system is hopelessly complicated. It made us feel, however, that we had got beyond the pale of civilisation, and we never attempted after this to do any purchasing ourselves, but were fortunate enough to be able to leave our money matters with perfect confidence in Mr. Ku's hands. The result was that we did our journey much more economically than other similar travellers, and were saved all worry.

It may be of interest to the reader to see one of the latest Government edicts on the subject of the currency, and to know that it has decided in favour of a uniform tael, the value of which is fixed at the astonishing figure of 1549 cash. According to the reports of the governors of the eighteen provinces, there were eleven provinces in favour of the tael as against eight in favour of the dollar currency. As the tael has never existed in coin form, and dollars are largely used, there is much to be said in favour of the latter; but the Chinese stick tenaciously to their own peculiar belongings, and in all financial transactions with foreign countries the tael has been the term used in the past.

The following edict appeared in the *Peking Gazette*, October 5, 1908:

"An Imperial Decree in response to a memorial of Prince Ching and other Ministers of the Government Council, and of Prince P'u-lun and other Members of the Senate, who, in obedience to our Commands, have deliberated upon the subject of a uniform national currency.

"A standard currency is the fundamental principle of public finance, and various countries have adopted a gold coin as their unit of value, with the subsidiary currency of silver and copper tokens. Under well-framed regulations such currencies have been found convenient and profitable. But it requires years of preparation to be ready for such a measure, which can by no means be attained at one step. The finances of China are in confusion, and the standardising of the currency is an urgent necessity. If actual gold coin were to be taken as the standard unit, it would be difficult to raise the necessary amount; while if gold were merely taken nominally as the standard unit, grave dangers would be incurred. It is evident, therefore, that we should first standardise and render uniform the silver currency, and then carefully proceed to take measures for a further advance; with a view to assuring the adoption of a gold standard in the future.

"The memorialists have pointed out that the use of the tael and its fractions has been so long established that it would be difficult to substitute any other denomination in its place. The Committee of Finance in a previous memorial also recommended the determination of the tael as the silver coin to be used.

"We, therefore, command that a large silver coin shall be struck weighing one K'up'ing tael, and that large quantities of silver coins weighing .5 of a K'up'ing tael shall also be minted for general convenience in use. Also there shall be small pieces of one mace and of five candareens, of less pure silver, which will serve as subsidiary currency. The two silver coins aforesaid shall be .980 fine, while the two small silver pieces will be .880 fine.

"This silver currency, except in so far as calculations under treaties and agreements with the Foreign Powers will require to be made as before, shall be uniformly used by all Yamens, great or small, in Peking or the provinces in all their Treasury transactions, and all allowances for differences of weight or touch, or meltage fees, &c. &c., shall henceforth be perpetually forbidden.

"Let the Governors-General and Governors of Provinces examine the conditions in their jurisdictions, and devise means in conjunction with the Board of Finance for determining afresh, either by increasing or decreasing as the case may be, the allowances and rice money of territorial authorities and tax-collectors while on duty, together with the expenditure for travelling on the public service, and let the rates be published openly by proclamation, so that the speculations of clerks and Yamen runners may be abolished for ever.

"As regards the diversity of silver currency in the various provinces, and differences of touch, which give dishonest traders and market-dealers the opportunity for demanding discounts and profits off each transaction, grievous injury is inflicted thereby on all classes, and the Board of Finance is now commanded to issue stringent regulations forbidding such practices in the future, with the view that in a given number of years the national silver currency may become completely uniform.

"Until the new coinage has been minted in sufficient quantities, the dollar and subsidiary silver pieces in use in the provinces, as well as the sycee, may be used as before, for the time being, on the market; and Treasury payments may still be made in sycee for the present, but must year by year be diminished by the substitution of the new silver coinage. On these questions let the Board of Finance carefully consider the circumstances and take satisfactory steps for the execution of this measure.

"Let this Decree be generally circulated in all parts.

"Memorial of the Government Council (Hui I Cheng Wu Ch'u) on the question of a Uniform National Currency."

To return to our subject: we made our way along the shingly beach, covered with large loose boulders, past the meat-market, where goats stood ready to be converted into mutton "while you wait," up to a broad platform of masonry, about twenty feet high, from which the trackers haul the boats up the rapid. They must have been certainly a quarter of a mile distant, and it takes about half-an-hour for some 60 or 100 men to get a heavy junk up the rapid—about 100 yards. We waited our turn from 7.30 A.M. till 5.30 P.M., and there were only thirteen boats ahead of us.

We found we had a short walk to the red-boat, but the men were so nice, and had rigged up the awning for us, and were so anxious that we should be comfortable and rest, that although we felt exasperated at having left our boat and our meal so unnecessarily early, we could not be angry with them. The red-boat was exquisitely clean, and the men clever, daring, and trustworthy: the captain was very tall, and had his head tied up because of a swelling, which made him look particularly interesting.

We sent Liu to procure provisions, as our last fowl had just been put in the pot, and he returned with three live ones (which appears to be the Chinese equivalent to a pair), price 2s. 3d. The fowls took

French leave to dine on persimmons, which had been left within reach, casting a furtive glance at intervals to where the boy was sitting meditating on the bank. The day gradually wore away, and we were very tired with the deafening noise of drums, guns, crackers, and shouting, without which accompaniment the junks could not be towed up the rapid in safety! The men on board yell and wave their arms as if in frantic desperation to scare away the evil spirits. At last our turn came, and our boat rode triumphantly up the rapid by means of two towing-ropes in the space of ten minutes. Ten hours' wait for a ten minutes' job! China certainly needs patience. Our men evidently thought they had done enough for the day: they tied up to the bank, and were soon snugly snoring for the night. They lie like rows of sausages, so tightly packed that it hardly looks possible for one to turn in his sleep, unless they did like seven sisters whom I know. When they were young and the house was full, they slept in one capacious bed: when one got tired and wanted to turn over, she said "turn," and all the seven had to turn together!

One of the men groaned heavily for some time, and then began to weep. This was too much for the others, who put an effectual stop to it, so that he groaned no more. In the morning I looked for the culprit, but no one looked particularly ill, as many are opium-smokers and always look a horrible dead colour.

The scenery grows grander and grander as you go

up the gorges, and the vicious-looking tide grows more and more threatening. Passing wrecks from day to day is by no means reassuring, but when one sees the slender rope on which the weight of a heavily laden junk depends, the marvel seems that any escape being wrecked. To the traveller who enjoys a spice of danger and loves glorious scenery no trip could be more attractive than a journey up the Yangtze for a month or six weeks, and it is quite easy to go almost the length of the empire by it. The return journey is performed in a very short time, and is certainly not lacking in excitement; for the boats seem to fly past us, and all hands on board are needed to keep the junk at all head foremost; while steering is a work demanding the utmost coolness, strength, and intrepidity, for the river is full of hidden rocks. The change in the height of the water adds immensely to the danger and difficulty of navigation. For the journey downstream the masts are taken down, and on a large junk fifteen or more men are kept rowing as if for dear life; and even then the junk often threatens to be carried down sideways.

When there is a strong wind blowing it is wonderful to see how the boats go up-stream, despite the current, while the men sit down with beaming faces for a few minutes' rest, or seize the opportunity to do a little washing. One merry fellow—the wag of the party—explained in pantomime that he wanted to see the soap with which we wash our hands, and was delighted when we gave him a little bit with which to wash a

VILLAGE AND JUNK

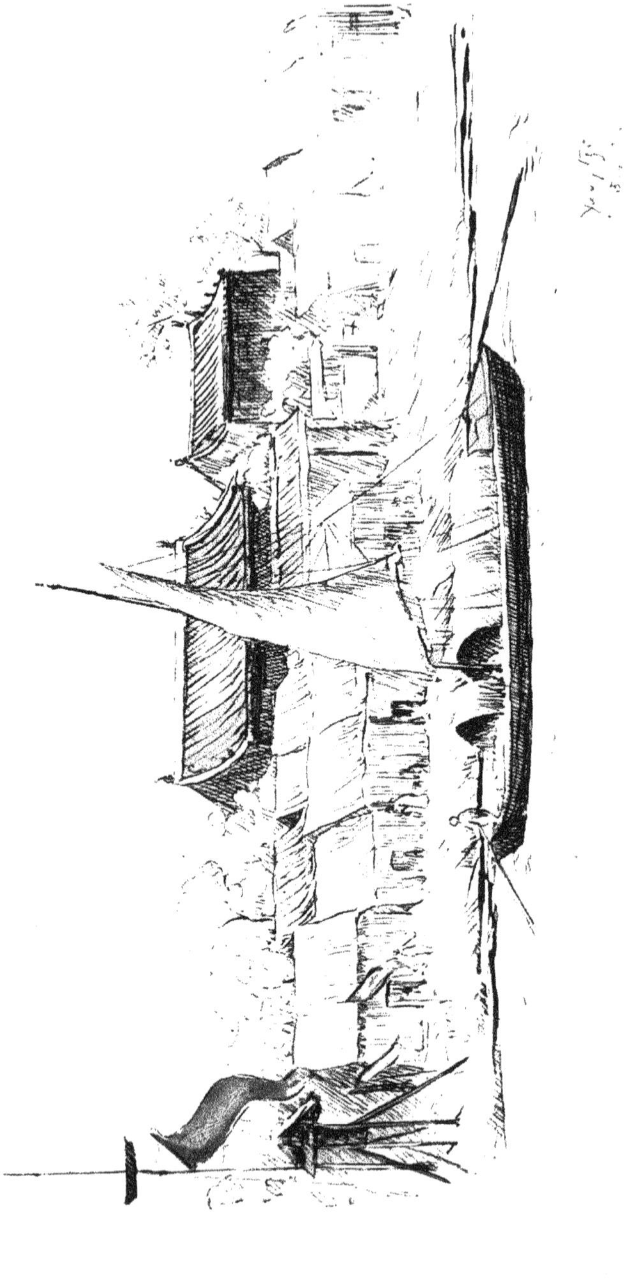

piece of cotton that he wraps round his head. They use very hot water but no soap for washing, and it is astonishing to see how clean they succeed in making their things. The tracker's next bit of work was philanthropic to a degree! He carefully washed out his mouth, then filled it again with water and applied it to a gathering on the sole of the foot of another man, and began to draw out the pus. I put a stop to it, however, and attended to the foot in a more Western manner. This was the beginning of my looking after the various sores of our party, and from this time on I rarely lacked patients. It soon became rather ludicrous, for any one who got a scratched finger seemed to think it required my attention, and I much regretted not having supplied myself with a dresser's case and a few simple requisites. Directly the man had had his foot attended to, he had to go on shore to track, with nothing but a straw sandal to protect the foot from stones and dirt. The endurance of the men is extraordinary, but happily they are insensitive to pain. A few days later a man came to me with a dreadful foot, swelled to almost double its proper size, and it was with great difficulty that I got the captain to allow him to stay on the boat instead of tracking (for *one* day), as he would have forfeited his wages for the whole trip if he were unable to fulfil his duty on a single occasion.

At intervals we passed small hamlets, and boats came alongside with various eatables, or charcoal, for sale. Half a pig was eyed most longingly by the men, and eventually they secured the head for a ridiculously small number of cash—exactly how many farthings they paid I could not see. Five pomeloes were to be had for one farthing apiece, and the cook was glad to get a fresh supply of charcoal. He spends the livelong day in his well—I do not know how else to describe it—with only his head and shoulders above the level of the deck. Close at hand is the drum on which it is his duty to beat instructions to the trackers when they are ashore. He is a most attractive subject for sketching, but is never still a moment except when he takes a nap, and then his head also disappears into the well, and he curls up, so that only his toes are visible. In my little sketch of him enjoying the fruits of his labour his long nails look like talons, and this is invariably the case when the nails are allowed to grow long: they are singularly repulsive, and the long silver nail-sheaths used by the gentry to conceal them are to be commended.

The days on the river slipped by very quickly, as there is always something fresh to watch, and if not rapids to go up every day, at all events there are difficult bits of navigation, and a certain anxiety attends the rounding of corners, when the current twists round with a threatening snarl. The picturesque villages make one long to stop and sketch, but one has to be content instead to try and jot down notes while passing alongside them. The accompanying sketch shows a typical one: the red flag was in honour of a royal birthday. A similar village is

THE LOOK-OUT ON THE YANGTZE

sly
ings
to be
glad

to

hich only
he deck.
duty to
e ashore
ing, but
n a nap
well,

variably
w long

a typical
royal birthday

ackers
sub-

disap-
his
ying
ions,

sive,

ly.
not
diffi-
attends
twists
que
one
notes
companying
was in
village is

Kweichow (Hupeh), quite near the big town of Kweichow Fu (Szechwan). It lies along the high bank, and the lofty city wall extends in a sort of wide semicircle up the bank above it, enclosing quite a large space of cultivated ground on the upper side of the town. The gates are closed at night, and no one can go in or out after the keys have been carried to the magistrate's yâmen.

On the ninth day after leaving Ichang we came to a village which in the distance we took to be on fire, owing to the dense clouds of smoke rising from it. It proved, however, to be one of the famous salt-springs, and had only emerged from the river-bed about a week earlier, owing to the fall of the water. The people had at once set to work erecting huts alongside it, and preparing the salt for use; and they live there till the spring, when the rise of the river drives them up the bank again. These salt-springs are one of the most valuable products of the province, but the principal ones are nearer the centre of Szechwan, and they are all a Government monopoly. Dr. Macgowan states—as an illustration of the extraordinary patient perseverance of the Chinaman—that it takes forty years in some cases to bore a salt-well.

Close to this village is the picturesque city of Kweichow Fu, extending some distance along the river-bank, with temples and palaces, and a Union Jack flying over a mission-house, which rises high above the city wall. The steep slope below it, from which the river had so recently subsided, was already ploughed ready for a crop of corn. The Chinese seem always on the watch to use every inch of ground available for cultivation: they never seem to lose an opportunity, or to grudge any amount of trouble. We climbed up the bank and a flight of steps, leading through a lofty gateway into the town. The streets were narrow and dirty, and thronged with people; but we turned aside to the attractive Union Jack, where we met with a warm welcome, even before we announced that we were bringing up belated stores from down the river. We set out almost immediately to visit an interesting palace, belonging to an Earl who had become famous during the Taiping war—a case of "la carrière ouverte aux talents." The façade and walls of the palace were curiously decorated with mosaic, formed from broken bits of pottery. There are shops for the purchase and sale of broken china and earthenware for this express purpose.

On entering the courtyard we saw handsome square gilt tablets—the gift of the Emperor to the late Earl—which were set up corner-wise over the entrance to an inner courtyard. At the farther end of this second court was a sort of reception-room, entirely open in front, containing chairs and tables and other beautiful furniture from Canton, a series of family portraits, and an ancestral tablet, with incense sticks burning in front of it. On either side of this room were doors leading into the living-rooms of the family. We wandered through side courts into the spacious garden, laid out in true Chinese style, with little stucco fountains and pools and streams, and many summer-houses, all furnished with couches for the guests attending opium-smoking parties. There were many kinds of shrubs and trees, some brought from long distances; also pomelo and orange trees laden with fruit. A beautiful oblong tank was full of lotos plants, and had a tiny boat on it; but over everything brooded the sadness of decay and the memory of a departed glory.

As we stood talking to the brilliantly dressed daughters of the house, a young cousin came in, who spoke excellent English, having been trained at St. John's College, Shanghai, and he proved to be a friend of Mr. Ku's. He offered to take us round to his father's palace, which was close by. It is built on exactly the same plan, and was in every way similar to the other; but we noticed one curious object in the reception-room—a large rough stone behind a screen under the ancestral tablet. This, he told us, was a stone used for divination in time of war, and above it was a most curious diagram hanging on the wall, representing men riding on tigers (=soldiers). There was also a scroll hanging on the opposite wall, given to the family by the Emperor after the death of the young man's father, recording the eminent deeds which he had performed. Among the curios which he showed us were some wooden ornaments formed out of little shrubs, which had been trained to grow into peculiar shapes, such as a lion, an old man, &c.;

these are particularly admired by the Chinese. Some parts of the decorations were quite charming in colour and in design, as for instance the double doors, decorated with golden bats on a dark-green background, and the gargoyles, formed like fishes, carved in stone. Altogether it was a fascinating place and a worthy setting to the courtly gentleman, who entertained us hospitably and took us round with his son. Unfortunately, his English was almost as limited as our Chinese. I should have very much liked to do his portrait, but dusk was coming on and we were leaving early next morning.

Two rather dreary days succeeded, as there was a west wind blowing, which took all the colour out of the landscape, just as an east wind does at home, and at the same time it added colour to one's temper. There is really much sense in the old French law, which prescribed special leniency of judgment in the case of murder and suicide committed when the mistral was blowing. Sketching was out of the question, and the poor trackers had a hard time—no rest all day long, for the wind was blowing dead in our teeth. We laboriously won our way up some small rapids, but nothing important was gained and we travelled very slowly.

The last rapid before Wanhsien is the worst, and as usual we got out, despite the reassuring news that, owing to the considerable fall in the level of the water, we should have an easy ascent. Our luggage was hastily transferred to the red-boat—as we imagined, to be taken ashore as usual—and we then landed, to allow our boat to start at once, for there were no other boats waiting ahead of us. The red-boat men, however, got some of our men to help them, and started first. We stood on a rock watching her come bravely through the flood, and were in the very act of photographing her, when she seemed to stagger, the men gave a great shout, dropped the towing-rope, the water dashed over her, and she was whirled down the stream like an utterly helpless log. We were horrified to see her carried down and out of sight round a bend, and the thought of our luggage added not a little, I must admit, to our dismay. It was some time before the two men on board succeeded in getting her to the bank, for the large steering-oar in front had snapped, which was the cause of the disaster. Hence the shout to the men to loose the towing-rope, or she would have gone on the rocks. About an hour later the men came back to us, carrying our luggage, which was none the worse for the wetting; but they told us it would be impossible for them to accompany us any farther, as it would take some time to repair the damage. We regretfully took leave of them, as the men had quite endeared themselves to us by the kindness and courtesy with which they were always on the alert to render us small services. Only the night previous our men were noisy and quarrelsome, and I was obliged to remonstrate sharply. At once the red-boat captain came to my assistance, and restored peace instantaneously. I wrote a note of thanks to the general at Ichang for the captain to give him, with our visiting-cards, when he reported himself on his arrival. I also gave visiting-cards to the captain for himself, as nothing seems to please a Chinaman more than this small courtesy, together with a lump of silver to be divided with his crew, and he received them with a beaming smile and a military salute.

After the accident we strolled along the bank for some distance, waiting for our junk to come up, and were much amused by inspecting a river-bank village. The whole of it is built of the most flimsy materials, and put together so lightly that it can be taken down and moved to another spot at the shortest possible notice, according to the height of the river. Even the god's shrine is thoroughly perambulatory, and is dedicated to the god of the earth. Many of the shanties are lofty erections, but the walls and roofs consist entirely of mats hung on to poles, which are merely tied together and stuck into the ground. There was quite a good village street, containing a barber's shop, a butcher's, a draper's (where most attractive wadded quilts made quite a goodly show), a chemist's, greengrocer's, &c.

There were several delightful restaurants, with pretty bowls and natty cooking arrangements, which made us long to purchase and experiment with them instead of using our primitive stove, where my bread refused to rise, though I never failed with it at home. So far, it can only be considered successful for making

1. RIVER-SIDE SHRINE

2. THE CHEF ON THE YANGTZE

...iverside shrine...

The chef on the Yangtze.

poultices, but we eat a little of it daily, as there is no sort of bread which we should find palatable in this part of the empire. The counters of the restaurants had many tempting dainties displayed upon them, especially tiny saucers full of relishes; among them we saw several Escoffier sauce bottles, but no doubt the original contents had disappeared long ago!

The women of the place seemed nice and friendly and clean, and were dressed in the gayest colours of the rainbow; green, scarlet, blue, and black was quite an ordinary combination on one person. They wear tight wadded trousers to just below the knee, and from there to the ankle the leg is neatly bound. Often the legs are very thin, and look like sticks, while the out-turned tiny feet and stiff knees all combine to give the appearance of goats' legs. While I was sketching the little shrine one came and stood beside it, with a very evident desire to be included in the sketch. I at once took advantage of this unusual occurrence—they generally flee directly they see I am doing them—but as the spectators laughed at her, she kept folding her arms across her face. She had a large basket on her back, and many women carry their babies in this way.

As one gets farther west the climate changes—growing milder—and the vegetation is different. Beautiful groups of bamboos are frequently seen, and crops of sugar-cane in patches of vivid green suggest the month of May rather than December. You reach the native home of oranges, and they seem to have a better flavour than anywhere else.

Mr. Ku came to me with a long face one day, to say that he had been told that the natives of Szechwan were barbarians, "and do you not think that Liu and I had better wear suits of uniform?" We had no hesitation as to the answer—a decided veto, having already discussed the question of carrying firearms, many of our friends having strongly urged us to do it. I am more than ever convinced that it is apt to lead to trouble, rather than avert it, and that it is safer to have none, especially when you have not been thoroughly trained in the use of them. My friend suggested that if you shot one Chinaman there would be ten to kill you, and a smile would be at least as efficacious as a revolver.

The last part of our river journey was rather disturbing, owing to our twice dashing upon the rocks; but happily no serious damage was done, and we had an excellent opportunity of seeing how these people set about repairs. The water was coming in rather fast under the floor of our cabin, so the carpenter took up the boards, baled out the superfluous water, and stuffed the hole with cotton wadding, which he extracted from his winter coat. This he adjusted neatly in the hole by means of his chopstick, and finally put a plaster over it, composed of the sole of an old shoe, which he tore up for the purpose, and nailed it over the spot. A good deal of baling had to be done, and no sooner was order restored in the cabin than we had a second collision, and the flooring had to be taken up again to see if there was any fresh mischief. Happily there was none.

Two sets of our friends have each been wrecked three times this season on their way up the river, and on one occasion the boat broke completely in half. Every one hastened to save what they could, except a Chinaman, who was observed busily washing his clothes with the soap that was oozing out of one of the cases of stores ! No goods are worth insuring on the Yangtze, as the insurance rates are so high, and it is so difficult—often impossible—to prove what has been lost. In the case when the boat was a total wreck, our friends were obliged to encamp for a week on the river-bank in a hut which they constructed out of their stores and luggage, with the sail of the boat spread over the top by way of roof—a somewhat ineffectual one when the rain came pouring down.

The river-banks are studded with temples, pagodas, and shrines, and the people in this part of the country are far more assiduous in their worship than anywhere else : we continually noticed them offering incense or paper money to the gods. The temples are less interesting than in the north, and ugly in colour, mostly a cold grey ornamented with black and white, and they are also less artistic architecturally.

On the fourteenth day we reached Wanhsien, whence we had decided to travel overland, though we were sorry to miss seeing the celebrated salt-wells, which we should have passed if we had taken the other more frequented route to Chengtu. We regretfully said good-bye to our boatmen, and made the eighteen men thoroughly happy and content with a gratuity of 7s. to be divided amongst them. We notice that the Chinese always seem more pleased and satisfied when they get the usual tip than when they get more. Wanhsien looked doubly attractive to us from the fact that we saw a British gunboat lying on the farther side of the river, but in itself the town is eminently picturesque, though dirty. A camel-back bridge, spanning a stream just before it entered the Yangtze, was perhaps the prettiest bit of all. Below it were endless yards of cotton hanging out to dry, after being dyed. This was a sight with which we soon became familiar, passing through many a village where the main street was draped in this way.

CAMEL-BACK BRIDGE

we ha... when the other
Chengtu. We regretfully
and made the eighteen
content with a gratuity
them. We notice that
pleased and satisfied
than when they get
ibly attractive to us
British gunboat lying on
but in itself the town is
dirty. A camel-back
before it entered the
est bit of all. Below
hanging out to dry,
a sight with which we
rough ... a village

CHAPTER XIV

Szechwan High-roads

SOME friends who preceded us up the Yangtze had arranged for sedan-chairs to be made in readiness for our arrival, so we were able to start on Monday morning at 7.45 on our journey to Chengtu, the capital of the province of Szechwan. We made quite an imposing array. The party was arranged as follows: first, two soldiers (our military escort); then my chair carried by four men; my friend's ditto; Mr. Ku's chair carried by two men, as it was a much lighter one than ours; then Liu's, which was a similar one (servants are always supposed to walk, but as Liu was from Peking, and totally unaccustomed to walking, we thought it best to let him ride); then came four coolies carrying luggage (each man reckons to carry 107 lbs.); and a head coolie, who is responsible for all the others, brought up the rear. The total cost of the seventeen coolies for fourteen days was 90,100 cash (£9), and the soldiers each received 2½d. per day wine money. The soldiers were most attentive, and would hardly leave our side except to go ahead and engage a room in the inn and have it made ready for us—namely, swept out and clean mats put on the bedsteads. They kept an eye on the luggage, though that is really unnecessary when there is a head man, as it is his duty, and he is responsible for everything. It is only when you have as many as fifteen coolies that a head man is considered requisite, but it is a great advantage in any case to have one.

The military escort is practically compulsory in this part of the country, for things are not very settled, though foreigners are much better treated than they were a few years ago. Our soldiers were most assiduous in their attentions, rushing to fetch hot water the moment we arrived at an inn, and eager to wash up our plates after meals, although we had a servant whose main duty it was to do this.

We had been told that Szechwan was flat, so we had a pleasant surprise in finding that our route lay almost the whole way through hilly, not to say mountainous country, and that the mountains were beautifully wooded. On the second day we reached Liang Shan, a pretty little town in a valley surrounded by steep hills; and after we left it the scenery was particularly beautiful. We passed through a thick forest of bamboos, whose pale, graceful, feathery foliage contrasted finely with the tall, dark pine-trees. The way led straight up a precipitous mountain by thousands of well-made stone steps. It seemed as if we should never reach the top, and the coolies must have thoroughly appreciated the fact that we were British travellers, and not Chinese; for the Chinese sometimes walk down-hill when it is very steep, but rarely indeed up-hill. When we asked Mr. Ku if he were accustomed to walking, he said, "Oh yes, I can walk two and a half miles," so evidently that is considered a long distance. In reality he proved to be a first-rate walker, and was soon able to do several hours a day without fatigue. The banks were full of all sorts of lovely ferns and mosses, reminding us of the most beautiful ferneries (under glass) at home; but here was of course the charm of nature instead of art. There was evidently a great variety of flowers in the spring-time; masses of orchids, and anemones, violets, and other plants we recognised, but there were far more whose species were unknown to us.

When we reached the summit at last there was a wonderful panoramic view of hill and plain as far as the eye could reach; miles upon miles of shimmering rice-fields, with trees and farmsteads reflected in them. A ceaseless stream of coolies passed us, carrying various kinds of loads suspended from each end of long sticks, which they carried across their shoulders. The loads were mainly baskets, paper, coal, hand-warmers, and pottery in this district. The hand-warmers are very neat; they are made of bamboo baskets containing a little earthenware bowl for charcoal. The people sometimes sit on them, or carry them in their hands, or even hang them under their coats, either before or behind—which at first aroused our pity, for we took them to be suffering from some terrible growth!

The Szechwan inns are not at all to our taste, nor do they compare favourably with those of Shantung, being mostly in bad repair and with paper hanging in shreds from the window-frames. There are large holes in the floors—mainly used for emptying slops through, on to the pigs living below—and decidedly perilous to the unwary traveller. The month of December, however, is the best time for visiting these inns, as the rats are then the only active foes; but they are painfully bold. I turned a sudden gleam of electric light from my private lantern on one of the rats in the middle of the night and startled him a good deal, but the scare wore off all too soon. Hosie has translated a Chinese verse which he met with in a Szechwan inn, and added a second one of his own. He says that the Chinaman's own description errs on the side of leniency, and I think he is quite correct.

"Within this room you'll find the rats
At least a goodly score;
Three catties each they're bound to weigh,
Or e'en a little more.
At night you'll find a myriad bugs
That stink and crawl and bite;
If doubtful of the truth of this,
Get up and strike a light.

Within, without, vile odours dense
Assail the unwary nose;
Behind the grunter squeaks and squeals
And baffles all repose.
Add clouds of tiny, buzzing things,
Mosquitoes—if you please,
And if the sum is not enough,
Why, bless me! there are fleas."

After passing through most beautiful scenery for five days, we came to a comparatively dull part of the country. Still, there were plenty of interesting things to look at, and continually something fresh which we had never seen before. The women wear very prettily embroidered clothes (worked in a sort of cross-stitch), though often appallingly dirty; and the clothes of the little children are lavishly decorated with delightful designs of butterflies and animals, and monsters, besides having worked pockets. I actually saw a toddler with a pocket-handkerchief, but I am convinced he did not know the proper use of it. If only there were not such a terrible dearth of these everywhere! I presented some to Liu as a New Year's gift, but the result was not altogether satisfactory, as the gift did not include lessons in the use of them.

It was only at the close of five days' journey from Wanhsien that we met the first beasts of burden (other than human ones). They were all cattle, and there were quite large numbers of them, neatly shod with straw sandals like those which the men wear. The crops were much more advanced here, and we even saw a field of beans in full flower. There is a good deal of corn, some peas and sugar-cane, but most of the land is devoted to the growing of rice, and is under water at the present season of the year. These fields are not large, and on each narrow little bank enclosing them there is a fringe of beans planted. The mandarin oranges grow extremely well, and are of a most lovely colour. The trees are often so heavily laden that they look as if they would break under the strain. Every wayside stall has quantities of oranges for sale at a merely nominal price. One cannot but suppose they are indigenous, and they certainly require little or no cultivation. The houses in this part look very pretty with their lath and plaster walls and overhanging eaves, but they are bare and dreary inside, as they rarely have any windows ; what little light penetrates comes from the door and from holes in the roof. The high-road has a most curious way of running straight through the houses (mostly restaurants), as seen in the accompanying sketch, in which also it may be noticed that the smoke issues from cracks in the walls. Chimneys are conspicuous by their absence throughout the empire. I think this may be the reason why photographs of Chinese towns look so unreal to us. Sometimes you think as you pass through a doorway that you are entering an inn, whereas it proves to be a village street, completely covered in by mats, stretched on rods from roof to roof, and making the streets quite dark in broad daylight.

The people seem friendly and good-tempered, and we passed one day through a district where nearly all the women had unbound feet ; but this is the only one I have ever come across in north, south, east, or west. Even the women working in the fields have bound feet, and it is astonishing how fast they are able to get about and what an amount of work they do. To be sure, they often carry little stools to sit on while they are weeding or planting in the fields. Sometimes they have a baby tied on their backs, but not infrequently this duty is relegated to the children, and you may

SZECHWAN HIGHWAY

see a toddler of not more than four or five years old carrying another nearly as large as himself, and trying to soothe its cries by swaying to and fro.

We found it most important to keep to the regular daily stages while travelling in the interior, but sometimes this is impossible, and then the most villainous inns have to be faced. We were delayed by rain, which made the roads extremely slippery and difficult. My men fell no fewer than three times one day, and on one occasion they flung the chair heavily on its side, smashing the windows; happily, I escaped with only scratches. The glass windows should have been replaced at their expense, but, fortunately for their purses, I felt that it was safer to be without windows after such an experience.

On the slippery days we usually began by walking, and as we skirted the hillsides, gradually climbing upwards, for the greater part of the way the sounds of labour rising from the valley reached us clearly. Often a heavy hoar-frost lay on everything, and the sun had been up for some hours before it had power to dispel it. Nevertheless, fellow-travellers found it strong enough to warrant the putting up of European umbrellas. Certain foreign articles are increasingly used by the Chinese, and the umbrella is a special favourite. We, on the other hand—delighted with novelty and picturesqueness—had taken to Chinese umbrellas, which were certainly much prettier, though rather heavy. The enamelled basin is especially attractive to the Chinese, and is perhaps the most used of all foreign articles. A pair of English boots may frequently be seen fastened on to the luggage—I think they are too precious to be used on the high-road and are reserved for the cities—and we have met soldiers wearing European gloves as a curious addition to their very unofficial-looking dress.

Yesterday our men found it so warm that they entirely uncovered their right arms and shoulders, like the images of the Buddha. When the people want to take their coats off, they take off three, four, or five together, like a plaster, and put them on in the same way.

In this district the irrigation is done by means of large wheels worked like a treadmill by two or three men at a time, and there are great numbers of these wheels to be seen; but, as is so commonly the case, the custom is purely local, and we only saw them for a day or two. It seems to me as if it were specially characteristic of China to have customs and appliances confined to the most limited areas, outside which they are not to be seen. This adds very much to the interest of slow travelling, as it keeps you constantly on the watch, and you are rewarded by always seeing something fresh. The trying thing about it is that if you do not buy the thing you want directly you see it, most likely you will never have another chance.

It is amusing to watch the harvesting of the peanuts which is now going on. Owing to the clayey nature of the soil, it is impossible to sieve them as in Shantung, so whole families establish themselves in a field, attended by their poultry and pigs, which are picketed out over the surface of the ground. This has been already dug up and cleared by the gatherers, but the family gleans what has been overlooked, and the poultry and pigs again glean what they may have left. Little Chinese children sit in baskets, but at a very tender age they begin to share the toils of their elders. It is astonishing to see the loads of salt, coal, or fire-wood which some of these tiny creatures manage to carry with a manly energy. There must be a good deal of country life in this district, for there are numbers of nice-looking farms situated on the hill-tops (as in the sketch of "Sunlight and Mist"), surrounded by haystacks and vegetable gardens and clumps of the useful bamboo. The bamboo seems to be used for every possible purpose, and many of the implements made from it are as ingenious as they are simple. Take, for instance, the rake; one end of the bamboo rod is split, the ends bent, and a tiny bit of plaiting spreads the prongs out fan shape. A greater variety of baskets, too, is made from bamboos than I have ever seen elsewhere, and they are used for a much larger number of purposes than at home.

As we plodded along the rice-fields one morning, after about an hour's walk we came to a wayside booth, where our men stopped for their first snack of food, and some particularly fresh-looking eggs tempted us to join their meal. The salesman proceeded to poach them, and would have added sugar if we had not stopped him. Declining chopsticks, I was provided with a nice little pottery spoon, and my friend took possession of a saucer about the size of a penny (commonly used for sauce) for the same purpose. Long strings of mules passed us, carrying taxes in the shape of small basket-loads of bullion, accompanied by a military escort. The leading mules were gaily decorated with flags, showing that they were on government duty. The road was bad and slippery, and our men soon decided to shorten the day's journey by one-third, which we declined to allow, having already spared their strength by walking for several hours ; we agreed, however, to shorten the stage to a certain extent. The natural result was that we found a horrible inn with only two tiny rooms at our disposal, an inner one being already occupied by several people. We agreed to remain there only on one condition—that these people should be put elsewhere ; and we found the three cells were more than filled by ourselves and our staff. There were no windows, but there was plenty of ventilation. The house was like a large barn, the end of which was divided off by a thin partition, in the centre of which was a round door. This part was again subdivided into three cubicles. The outer part of the barn was like a big restaurant, and after a while the many inhabitants rolled themselves up like sausages in the wadded quilts provided by the inn, and bestowed themselves as comfortably as might be on tables or benches, and comparative silence reigned for a few hours. Happily, the rain stopped, for there was quite enough open space in the roof above my head and in the walls for us to study astronomy had it been a clear night. We found it unnecessary to have our pan of charcoal taken out at nights, for there was always a lovely breeze to carry away any fumes there might be.

In this district the beds are made of straw, covered with a bamboo matting, and are not uncomfortable; but we always felt happier when we got a plain wooden bedstead like a large, low table.

We passed a night at an interesting large town called Shun King Fu, and were greatly charmed with the lovely silks we saw being made there, and the silver work. Everywhere the people were busy with the various processes of silk-making. Hand-looms, of course, are used, and we saw the most exquisite golden shades of silk in all stages of manufacture. It is, however, never sold in its natural golden colour, or white (as that is the Chinese mourning), unless some European succeeds in getting hold of a piece in its unfinished state. Some of the natural dyes are wonderfully brilliant, but unfortunately none of them seemed to be fast colours. The red and yellow vegetable dyes and indigo are grown in the province of Szechwan, but, sad to say, aniline dyes have been introduced, and are becoming more and more common.

The missionaries who were entertaining us kindly sent out to a silk merchant to bring pieces for us to select from, as it is not very usual for ladies to go out shopping in this city. When we had chosen what we wanted, the silk had to be weighed, instead of measured, to ascertain what the price was. The merchant, who brought lovely embroidery silks for sale, had neat little scales in a case with which to weigh the skeins. A long discussion as to the price ensued, as it had gone up since our hosts bought similar silks a month before, and no valid reason could be produced for the change. Of course the system of bargaining is universal, and we were thankful to have some one to tell us what the price ought to have been and to do the bargaining for us. Next the silversmith was summoned, and he brought a trayful of various silver ornaments, ready to be inlaid with kingfishers' feathers. This is an art peculiar to China; in fact, no one but a Chinaman would have the patience requisite for doing it. The effect is that of the most brilliant, iridescent, blue-green enamel, and usually beads or red-coloured glass or coral are introduced instead of jewels. It is particularly effective when combined with jade. This jewelry was also sold by weight, and we had to leave our purchases to be "feathered" and sent after us, as everything of that sort is only made to order. Brides frequently wear a sort of crown made of silver and kingfishers' feathers, which looks extremely effective. There are some fine examples of this work in the Chinese Section of the South Kensington Museum.

We were told that we must make an early start next day, as it was a very long stage—between thirty and thirty-five miles—so we were up betimes, and ready at six o'clock. Luck was decidedly against us. First one of the coolies said he was ill and could not go, so another had to be got, which delayed us nearly an hour. The morning was very grey, and a cold drizzle soon set in. My chair-bearers fell down even before we got outside the city, and the road became more and more sticky every moment. The men hate cold water, and had to walk round every puddle, which took up a great deal of time. The ground is composed of a particularly sticky clay, which is perhaps the reason why not only the cattle but also the funny little black pigs wear straw sandals when they travel.

After our chairs had been upset more than once we decided that it was less unpleasant to walk, and the soldiers came valiantly to the rescue when the road was specially difficult, as in the case of long flights of slippery steps. Sometimes they gave us a hand, and sometimes they clutched an elbow to save us. The descriptions of slippery places and the perils of the road, as given in the Book of Psalms, were perpetually before our mental vision. Nothing could more accurately describe Chinese roads in wet weather. The coolies tied little metal things on to their sandals, which was somewhat of a help, but we felt almost thankful when at midday the rain settled into a steady downpour; for, though it was rather dreary, it was less slippery. There were a large number of chairs on the road, and some as important-looking as our own. This was the only bit of the journey when we travelled like mandarins, but we lacked the smart military uniforms of the mandarins' coolies; ours were the most disreputable, ragged-looking crew, and much less satisfactory as carriers than those we had in Shantung or Yünnan. In the nine days that we had been travelling from Wanhsien we had only once met a four-bearer chair, but now we were nearing the capital—Chengtu—the road was much more crowded with traffic of all sorts. The last stage of the journey is through comparatively level country. After a breakneck descent from the mountains we entered the plain in which Chengtu is situated. It is about ninety miles in length by forty broad, and has been well described as a garden. Colonel Manifold estimates that it contains a population of 1700 to the square mile, and there are seventeen cities in it. The old familiar groan of wheelbarrows greeted our ears once more, though the type is slightly different here from that of Shantung; they are much smaller and only accommodate one person, or (as we frequently saw) one fat pig, lying on his back, with his legs in the air. The seat is immediately behind the wheel, and it looks decidedly comic to see a woman, wearing tight pink trousers, with a leg cocked jauntily on either side of the wheel.

In this part of the country we passed through villages much more frequently, and the people had a busier air. There are markets held every few days in one or other of the villages, so that we continually met people coming from them laden with their spoils. They kept passing us on the road wearing paper caps

SUNLIGHT AND MIST IN THE MOUNTAINS

over their hats, and on inquiry we learnt that this was done to preserve their pristine freshness. The fields were full of people weeding, and they looked very comfortable, seated on their little stools, and with warming-pans between their feet ; for it was the week before Christmas, and the weather was growing cold. The minute kind of care the peasants here give to their crops is most interesting, each individual plant in a field being carefully attended to and manured. Each member of a family seems to share in the toil and to have implements suited to his or her size, some of them the "cutest" little weapons imaginable. The people look well fed and attended to, but their clothing is often a network of rags, and their houses are singularly dark and forbidding. If there is any scarcity through unfavourable crops, they suffer immediately and acutely, as agriculture is the most important industry of the province. The men have such long pipes that they frequently use them as walking-sticks. Often the women came round and smilingly interrogated us. Then we went through an amusing dumb conversation of the most friendly sort. The subject is usually the same—*feet*—and they never fail to admire our English boots, if not our feet. We, on our side, express much admiration of the exquisite embroidery of their shoes, though we do not admire *their* feet. Everywhere they seem to think we must be doctors, and they come and explain what a pain they have in the region of the digestion. We administer a harmless and comforting dose of ginger, and they swallow it with the utmost faith, which we hope may cause it to be doubly efficacious. In any case it is a sign of our goodwill, and establishes a friendly feeling among the people, and I do not see that it can do any harm.

We reached Chengtu on the morning of the fourteenth day, and spent a full hour wandering in search of the English missionary's house, on whose kind hospitality we were reckoning; for there are many missions in this large city, and our men at once made for the most imposing, which, needless to say, is American.

It may seem strange to people at home to hear that travellers habitually swoop down on missions, often without even giving notice beforehand, and are invariably welcomed with courtesy and kindness. Travelling in China would be a much more difficult matter than it is if it were not for the ungrudging helpfulness and hospitality of the missionaries. Those to whom we had been directed were unable to take us in, on account of illness, but had made arrangements for us to be entertained at the Friends' mission, and helped us in many other ways.

CITY GATE. CHENGTU

E. F. R.
Chêng-tu-fu.

CHAPTER XV

Chengtu

CHENGTU is unquestionably the cleanest city in China, and probably is the most progressive and enlightened of any purely native city. The streets are broad and well kept, and the foreigner can walk anywhere without the slightest fear of molestation. At almost every street corner there is a policeman, and many of them have sentry-boxes. They are neatly dressed in a sort of European uniform, and are decidedly clean and civil. They wear a kind of small black sailor-hat, and the smarter ones wear black thread gloves of native manufacture and carry stout walking-sticks. Altogether, they are the best type of police we met. There are no beggars with their hideous whine and incomparable dirt. This is a magnificent triumph for the head magistrate, as a few years ago they numbered twenty thousand in Chengtu; but he was determined to put an end to the system, and has entirely succeeded. We met a large school of boys neatly dressed, and were told that these were the children of the beggars, whom he had collected into a large school, where they are taught trades at the expense of the municipality.

On the day of our arrival a kind friend offered to

take us round the city. For the first time since leaving Shanghai, we found we could go on a real shopping expedition, and we had a glorious afternoon of it. It would be hard to find a more fascinating place than Chengtu for shopping. The curio shops had much that was attractive, though nothing of any great value. We were told that we must proceed with great caution if we wished to get things at a reasonable price; and fortunately we were able to discuss in an unknown tongue, which was a great advantage to us in dealing with the shopkeepers. Our method of procedure was as follows:—firstly, to look with interest at all the things we did *not* want, such as a baby's feeding-bottle or old beer-bottles; secondly, to point out all the flaws in anything that we *did* want, turning up our noses till they were nearly out of joint; thirdly, to ask the prices of many things, and to exclaim "Ai-ah" in an incredulous tone on hearing the price of the things that we wanted to purchase. Then we named a price about five times below what was asked. Finally we left the shop and strolled away up the street, while our kind friend further discussed the matter with the shopkeeper, we having previously arranged with him in English how high we were willing to go. On an average we got the things at about half the price named originally, but sometimes we got them considerably cheaper. There was not much old china to be seen, but a few bronzes and a good deal of interesting brass, mostly modern. Chengtu is a great place for the manufacture of horn things, especially lanterns, which are most ingeniously constructed. The sheets of horn are joined by being melted together, and Hosie gives a most interesting description in his trade report of the way that these and other things are made in Chengtu. There is a great manufacture of masks, and of whole heads of the same kind, which are painted brilliant colours, especially pink. In another street it is interesting to watch the sacred money being made. Outside each shop a tree trunk is set up about six feet high; the top of it is carved to form a mould, the shape of a silver shoe. Into this the paper—made from bamboo or rice straw—is beaten into shape with a hammer by a man standing upon the counter in order to reach up to it. The basket-shops, too, are most enticing, and here they make the largest baskets I have ever seen, about four feet high and about two yards in diameter. This is the place from which loofah comes; it is the inside of a peculiar kind of melon. Chengtu is the great trade centre, too, for spices and musk, furs, &c., which come from Tibet; but the great trade of the place is in silks, as in the days of Marco Polo—and these were brought to the house another day for us to see. The figured *crêpe de Chine* was beautiful, and the shades were different from those to be seen at home. I got a lovely figured brocade at about 3s. 9d. per yard, and *crêpe de Chine* at 1s. 6d. You can see these silks being woven in numbers of the dark-looking houses, and the design is made by a person sitting above the loom, almost in the roof. Another charming industry is that of ribbons and braids, which are made on the most ingenious little machines. The people sit outside their doors working at them, as you see the women with their lace bobbins in European countries.

The people seem a poor, cheerful, thrifty folk, and there is an air of prosperous activity throughout the whole city. Many parts of it are extremely picturesque, and there are beautiful trees of various kinds shading the wide thoroughfares. In the evening our attention was attracted by tall poles, with lights placed so high up that they could have been of no possible use to anybody. We found that they were put up by pious persons to light the "orphan spirits"—that is to say, to show the way home to people who had died away from their own city.

The following day we visited the famous Buddhist monastery, enclosed by a wall above which rose lofty trees. Passing through the fine entrance, we faced a large gilt Buddha in a narrow shrine ; back to back with this, and divided off by a thin partition, was another figure of the Buddha, facing the court. Here the Abbot received us most courteously, and sent for his secretary to show us round. The accompanying diagram shows the ordinary sort of arrangement both of temples and monasteries. The temples generally form a group of buildings separated from one another by courts one behind the other in a straight line, the principal buildings forming the ends, and minor buildings running along the sides of the courts. The hall of meditation of the monks was an imposing

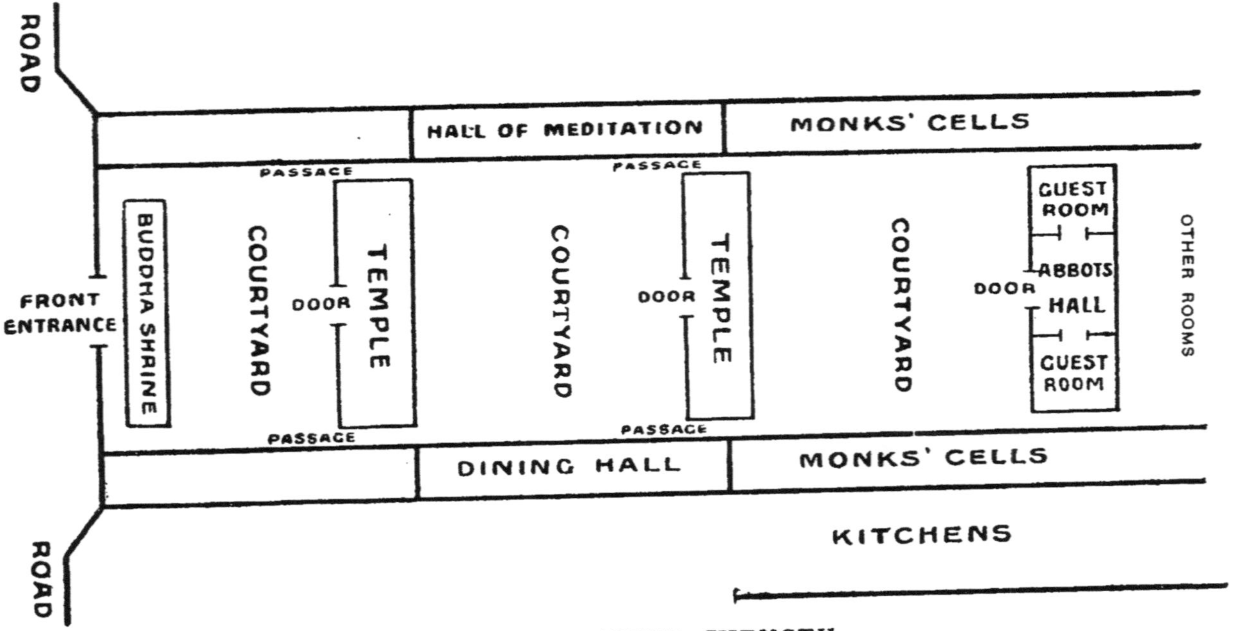

PLAN OF MONASTERY, CHENGTU

room with seats along the walls, on which the monks sit cross-legged, looking very much like Buddhas. Everything was beautifully clean in the dining-hall, which was filled with long tables, on which three bowls and a pair of chopsticks were placed at intervals for each monk. In the kitchen we saw an enormous boiler, where over a bushel of rice is cooked for each meal, to supply the appetites of a hundred and fifty monks. A large wooden fish acts as a gong for summoning the monks to meals, and another gong is used to summon them to tea.

One of the monks looked as if he had been recently branded for sainthood with nine marks about the size of threepenny-bits, symmetrically dotted over his skull. Hackmann gives an interesting description of the way this is done in his book *Der Buddhismus*. The candidate for sainthood has small pieces of incense fastened on to his shaven head by means of resin. These are lighted and allowed to burn into the flesh, while a chant is kept up by the other monks, and the sufferer has some one to press his temples with his thumbs to relieve the pain.

At the end of the third courtyard we were taken into a lofty temple, where the Abbot's throne faced the doorway. A gilt Buddha, with fruit and flowers placed on a table, formed a sort of altar in front of it. Round doorways, without doors, led to guest-rooms on either side of this hall, and we were hospitably entertained in one with tea and cakes. By permission of the Abbot, I returned next day to make a sketch of

BUDDHIST MONASTERY

ked for eac
ned and fift
for sum
her gong is use

had been recentl
ks about the siz
ed over his skull
tion of the wa
The candi

this picturesque interior, and in this sketch the doorway is shown, which is very characteristic of Szechwan architecture. Many of the inns in this province have circular doorways and windows. The Abbot came and talked with us very politely, and on inquiry I learnt that a most beautiful painting of lotus blossoms in black and white, which hung over the doorway, was by a celebrated artist, and had been presented to the monastery by a pious worshipper. The Abbot sat down and began discussing our respective religions, which he said were exactly the same. While agreeing as to their fundamental principle being the same, I felt unable to discuss their differences, being somewhat inattentive, I fear, owing to my endeavour to get on with the sketch as rapidly as possible. Next the Abbot was sure we must be hungry, though we had just been regaled with excellent sweets and tea, and, despite our refusing it, he insisted on sending us some of the meal to which he had been summoned. A monk soon appeared with bowls of vermicelli and greens. It was not unpalatable, and much easier to manage with chopsticks than might be supposed, as the bowl is held close to the mouth and the food shovelled in with chopsticks aided by suction. At intervals the novices came in to worship, and prostrated themselves before the altar. Most of the monks were dressed in pretty silver-grey robes, but some in the orthodox orange, and the Abbot wore a blue cloak. It was certainly an attractive community, a great contrast to those we saw in Peking.

Educationally Chengtu stands in the front rank of Chinese cities. Everywhere there are schools and colleges established on the new lines, and more are being built. The people are so enthusiastic that they have rather overshot the mark, it may be thought. In order to facilitate the girls' going to school they are being dressed as boys, so that they may pass through the streets unnoticed to attend the various schools which have been started for them. One girl came to a friend of mine to seek admission to her school, and not only did the European take her for a boy (telling her the boys' school was on the other side of the road), but so also did the Chinese gatekeeper, who insisted she had come to the wrong place. At the recent athletic sports the students put up a notice that no lady with bound feet would be admitted to the ground, and we hear that this notice is now being put up everywhere throughout the empire on such occasions. Anti-foot-binding is certainly making good progress among the upper classes, and we even saw a shoe-shop with large shoes for ladies prominently displayed on the counter. Nowhere else have we seen this.

There is a large military medical college at which there are three French doctors. Their presence is not altogether agreeable to the Chinese, and when one retired recently the officials took the opportunity of suggesting that he should not be replaced. They said that they could not afford his salary. How great must have been their disappointment when they were informed that their new professor had already arrived, and that the French authorities were quite willing to pay for him! Foreign competition in China has its funny side, but I marvel at the way the Chinese endure it.

The University is an interesting but eminently unpicturesque place, and the students are cramming Western subjects in a way to cause intellectual dyspepsia. As everywhere in China, English is the main subject, and they have a professor from Cambridge, with two English assistants and a Dane. French, German, and Japanese are also taught, and there is only one professor for Chinese classics. Sunday is a holiday, and many students spend the week-end at home. The walls of the class-rooms are nearly all window, but it is in no ways disturbing to Chinese students to have any number of spectators, or to be able to see into the adjoining class-rooms. Each study is occupied by three or four students, and the studies are simply partitioned corridors with a passage down the centre and a railing on either side of it, instead of walls. The dining-rooms are like outdoor restaurants with a roof over them, and the students sit four at a table. The fees for the year, including everything, are thirty dollars (about £3. 10s.). Many students are very anxious to study in England, but cannot possibly raise the necessary funds; and until proper arrangements are made to look after them when they do come, it is hardly a desirable plan. America is far ahead of us in this respect, and England would do well to follow her example. Everything is in our favour at present, and it might be of the utmost value as regards the development of China, and the commercial interests of England, to seize the opportunity of educating some of her ablest scholars. A Chinese gentleman told me that students returning from England are very apt to be full of bumptiousness because they have come out head of their class in English schools, while they have failed to assimilate what they have learnt. We spent an evening with some students, answering questions about the different countries we had visited. They wanted to know about the government, the religious and general conditions of other lands. Naturally the questions covered far too big an area to admit of satisfactory answers, but probably the men would have been willing to listen all night, if we had been willing to go on talking. They were most interested to hear the reasons why we admire China and the points of superiority which it possessed.

On the last day of the year the Viceroy and the Tartar general sent presents to all the foreign community. Their visiting-cards were brought in, and a list of the presents which were waiting outside—hams, pigeons, ducks, fruits, and sweetmeats. We went outside to see them, and found the presents displayed on trays on the top of large boxes, or hung round them. It is customary to select about two things; visiting-cards are sent back with the remainder, and a small present of money is given to the servants who bring the gifts. They replace what

MILITARY YAMEN

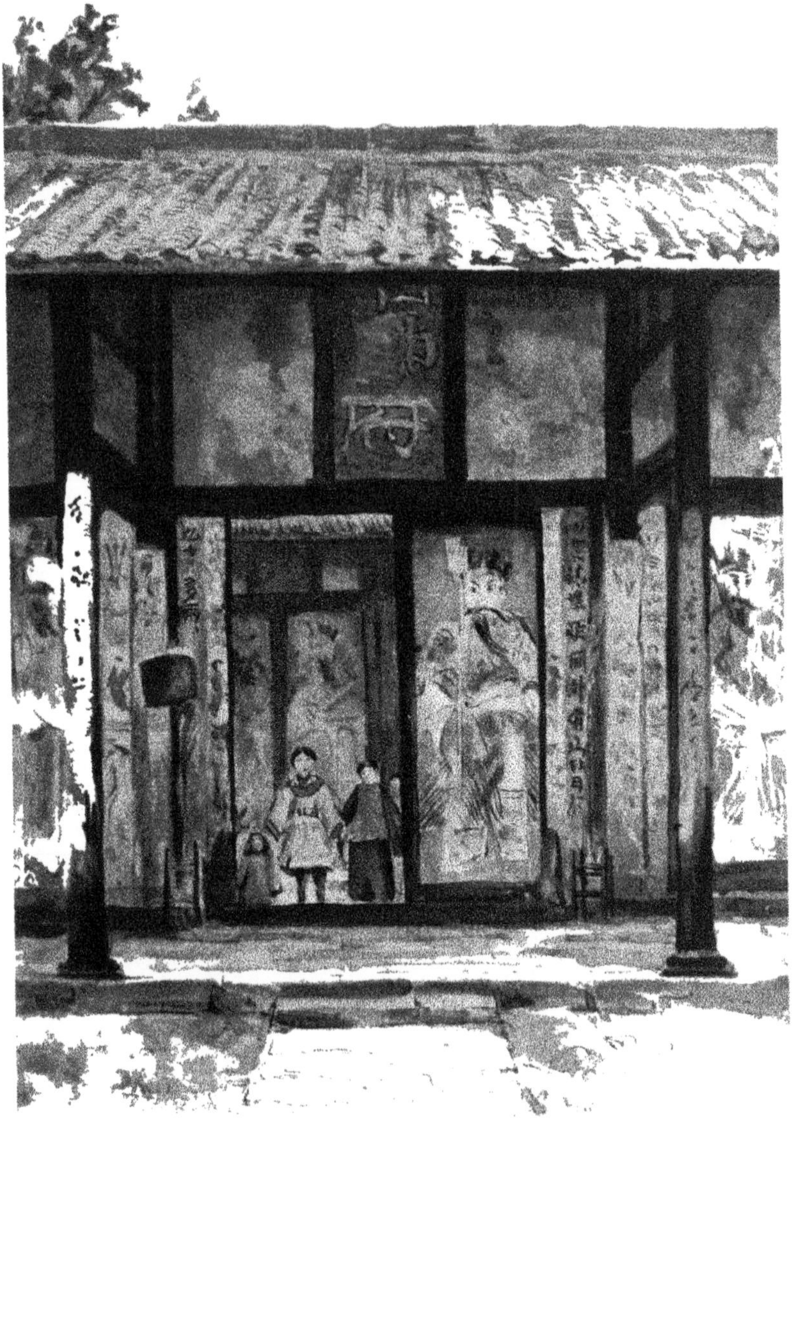

has been selected from a supply inside the box, and then carry them on to the next house. We went to see the Tartar general's yamen in the Manchu city, a very pretty spot embowered in trees, and quite typical of Chinese official buildings. The inscription over the entrance is "Yamen of the greatest General," and on the doors and walls are highly coloured pictures of the tutelary gods, two celebrated generals of the T'Ang dynasty (A.D. 618 to 905); one is white-faced, and the other red-faced. These pictures are repeated all along the wall, and also on the doorways of the inner courtyard, which in the sketch appears in the background. They are singularly ugly, but as the pictures of the door-gods are seen on the houses of all, even the poorest, the sketch of them may not be devoid of interest. On private houses some of them are quite little papers like advertisements, while again some of the private houses have large gilt figures covering the whole doors. One day we went outside the city to visit a fine temple, and came to a place where there is a road on which you can drive in carriages. This is the only place in the province where there is a carriage, but we did not have the privilege of seeing it. The walls are broad enough and smooth enough on the top to make a splendid carriage drive—four or five vehicles might easily drive abreast—and as they are ten miles round, it would really be a fine promenade. In the spring the view must be very beautiful, for there is a range of snowy mountains in the distance, and many branches of the Min River water the intervening plain. During the whole week that we spent at Chengtu we never saw the mountains, on account of the mist; but it was not hard to imagine the beauty of the place when the flowers are out and the brilliant butterflies hovering round them.

We took part in an interesting event while we were staying here—the purchase of land for a Christian university. Heavy bundles of silver "tings" had to be weighed before the payment was settled. Four different missionary societies have each agreed to build a college and to provide a certain number of qualified teachers. It is also proposed that Etonians should furnish a hostel. This university scheme for the west seems likely to be the forerunner of one also in the east of the empire, but the latter will be on more ambitious lines.

We were sorrier when the time came for us to leave Chengtu than we were to resume our journey on any other occasion. We had decided to go by river to Kiating, despite the fact that it was very low; and as we left the city we came to the wall where the new barracks are situated, and saw some soldiers doing the goose-step. Others were jumping into a trench, where nearly every one landed on all-fours. There was very great hesitation before they dared leap at all. The city is enclosed by one of the branches of the river, and we had not to go very far outside the wall before we reached the point where our boat was moored.

CHAPTER XVI

The Min River

WE reached the riverside—it looked merely a stream—and found our boat, with the luggage already aboard, looking most unpromising, despite the efforts of our men. It was a small river craft about eight feet broad. Bamboo matting not more than five feet high formed our house-room, with a few planks for a door in front. Fragments of matting made a partial screen in the centre. The floor was of a rudimentary character, just a few boards with large gaps between them, through which one could study the depth of water over which our luggage was precariously poised on low props. In order to prevent all our small things from dropping through the floor, we spread over it our invaluable sheets of oil-cotton (a kind of waterproof largely used everywhere in China), and fastened up a curtain at each end of the tiny boat to secure a small amount of privacy. There was just space for our two carrying-chairs and our mattresses. One of the chairs we used as a wardrobe, and the other as a store-cupboard. The bamboo chairs we had procured at the penitentiary of Chengtu, despite the advice of our friends, as we found sedan-chairs very irksome, and decided that open ones would be more comfortable and enable us to see the country better. With long fur coats and foot muffs we felt that we could brave the cold, and there was always the resource of walking if we got too chilly. We never for a moment regretted our decision, and we found that the men carried the open chairs far better than the heavy closed ones. We profited at once by the exchange, as they were able to be used for going to Mount Omi, and we were carried some distance up the mountain. Under the seat was a box in which we could carry all our small things, and the coolies hung their coats, hats, &c., on the back.

As our room was so small we sat mostly on the floor, so as to have everything within reach without getting up. The cooking was a somewhat difficult matter, as the brazier on which it was done was only six inches in diameter, and rather apt to burn a hole in the floor if it was heated sufficiently to do any cooking. We were glad of its warmth, as the weather was very cold. Chopsticks were evidently the correct fireirons, and are just the right size to match the charcoal. With practice I got fairly expert at making palatable dishes, as naturally the range of the menu was much limited. From this time onward I did all the cooking, and I cannot help attributing to this fact mainly the excellent health we enjoyed throughout the whole journey.

It was on his way from Chang Te to Mount Omi that the unfortunate Lieutenant Brooke was murdered by Lolos about a year later than we were there. We were strongly warned about the care requisite in dealing with Lolos, and told that it was imprudent even to mention the name in public, as it is considered a term of reproach. It was suggested that we should spell it if desirous of speaking of them. Their country is marked on the maps as "Independent Lolos," and covers about 11,000 square miles: no Chinaman dare penetrate into it without the safe-conduct of a Lolo. Their speech, dress, customs, religion, and laws are entirely different from those of the Chinese. No one has yet come into sufficiently close contact with them to ascertain even approximately the number of Lolo tribes in existence at the present time, speaking different dialects. What was true at the time that Baber explored Western Szechwan is equally true to-day—that practically nothing is known about them. He gives a graphic description of the Lolos whom he met, which I quote at length: "They are far taller than the Chinese; taller probably than any European people. During the journey we must have met hundreds of them, but we never saw one who could be called, even from an English standard, short or undersized. They are almost without exception remarkably straight-built, with thin muscular limbs. Their chests are deep, as becomes mountaineers: the speed and endurance with which they scale their native mountains is a prodigy and a proverb for the Chinese. Their handsome oval faces, of a reddish brown among those most exposed to the weather, are furnished with large, level eyes, prominent but not exaggerated cheekbones, an arched but rather broad nose, an ordinary mouth, somewhat thin-lipped, and a pointed and characteristic chin from which the beard has been plucked. The same process has denuded the upper lip, which is of good proportion. Their teeth are remarkably white and regular, a preservation for which they account by asserting that they never eat roast meat, but always boil their food. Perhaps the most marked character of their faces is a curious tendency to wrinkles, especially on the forehead, which is low, but broad and upright. The lowness of the features may be merely an illusive appearance, since it is overshadowed by a peculiar style of hairdressing. With very rare exceptions the male Lolo, rich or poor, free or subject, may be instantly known by his *horn*. All his hair is gathered into a knob over his forehead, and then twisted up into a cotton cloth, so as to resemble the horn of a unicorn. The horn with its wrapper is sometimes a good nine inches long." Baber mentions slave raids made by the Lolos to capture Chinese children, whom they usually bring up like their own children. They tattoo the slaves on the forehead with a blue cross. Apparently it is to have a place of safety in case of such raids that the Chinese have built towers like the one I have sketched on the borders of Yunnan. Many of the customs of the Lolos are peculiar and interesting, and the position of woman is far above that enjoyed in

China. The birth of a girl is more highly esteemed than that of a boy, and a stranger introduced by a woman Lolo has the best possible guarantee. Baber considered that a European would be quite safe in Lololand if properly introduced and of honest character. The most experienced and successful travellers always seem to emphasise the importance of the latter fact.

We were escorted by two soldiers, as usual. Our progress was far from rapid, as the river is extremely low at this season. For the first two days we were generally able to see to the bottom, and often we scraped the stones if we did not actually stick fast. The men seemed to spend nearly as much time in the river, pushing and pulling us, as on the boat. It was a picturesque and interesting journey, as we continually came to the dams made for irrigation purposes. We much regretted that we were unable to visit Kwan Hsien (thirty-six miles north of Chengtu), where the system of irrigation of the plain can be seen at its source. As we were short of time, and also heard that we should not see much at this time of the year, it did not seem worth while going there. The Min River flows from the Min Hills, and just near Kwan Hsien a cutting was made in order to divide it into two large branches. These again were subdivided into many others, forming a network to irrigate the whole of the plain in which Chengtu lies. This was done by an able governor more than 200 years B.C., and the original system, which is still in use to-day, has turned an unproductive plain into one of great fertility. Naturally, there have been many improvements made in the course of centuries, and dams and dikes have been erected to regulate the flow of water. We were able to see quite a number of these after leaving Chengtu, and to marvel at their simple and successful construction. They are mostly made of bamboo crates, filled with stones, and rising about three feet above water. These are placed in long lines, and the temporary dike is made of sand. The channels have to be cleaned regularly, and large sums have to be spent on repairs. The farmers pay a tax of about ½d. an acre, and, in order to get the money in regularly, they are compelled to pay double if it is not paid before a certain date. For about a month yearly the river below Chengtu is closed, and there is always a great crowd of boats at that time, both above and below the dam, waiting for the re-opening. The opening of a big dam, such as the "Frog's Chin," is an imposing ceremony, preceded by a day of worship at the temples and the inspection of dikes. All the officials attend, and when the sluice is opened the runners of the officials lash the water, and the women and the children throw stones in to make the water run faster to irrigate the fields!

Throughout the plain there are many water-wheels to raise the water to higher levels, and some also are apparently used for grinding corn. At the close of our first day's journey on the river there was a great

HOUSE ON MIN RIVER

deal of loud talk when we halted for the night, added to the tiresome beating of the drums by the night watchmen, who patrol the towns and big villages all night long. It turned out that a man had come to try and persuade our captain to undertake a bigger job than ours. On being warned that the interpreter would hear what he said, he remarked that it did not matter, as he would not be able to understand the dialect. Mr. Ku, however, had studied the dialect when he was at college, and thoroughly understood the plan that was being devised. This was that we should slip down the river in the middle of the night, while the escorts were away sleeping at the inn. Then some story would be trumped up that the boat could not take us any farther, and we should have been obliged to find another one. Mr. Ku had the good sense to go ashore at once and apply to the Yamen for a couple of soldiers to come and sleep on board, so that there was no opportunity for the captain to undertake the new job even if he had been willing to do so, and we had no further trouble. Certainly, one could hardly be surprised if the captain wished to make a little more money, for he receives about 6s. for a trip which lasts four days, and out of this money he has to pay and feed two other men besides feeding our two. We hear that a man can live (without starving) on a penny a day for food, and the regular allowance of soldiers is only 2d. per day.

We passed many picturesque villages, some built in lath and plaster, which, at a little distance, might almost have been taken for Cheshire villages, if it were not for the beautiful blue figures flitting about; for blue is the universal colour of the clothing here. We were much interested to see a large number of fishing cormorants at one place; but unfortunately they were not at work. Very light rafts are used for this purpose, turned up at one end, as in the sketch. We also twice saw otters used for the same purpose. The Chinese declared to us that the otter brings the fish up in its paws, and not in its mouth; but they always invent an answer so glibly to your question, whether they know the answer or not, that I should certainly not believe the above without further corroboration. We were surprised to see in one place that the cormorants (after diving) were fished up to the surface in baskets very much the same shape as the birds, and evidently made for the purpose.

About forty miles below Chengtu, the two main branches of the river unite and form something more worthy of the name of river. The branch which flows through Chengtu is called the "Walking Horse River" at its division from the main current—a very dangerous spot for navigation, and one where there are constant disasters. It is said that the rafts generally carry coffins with them in consequence; and certainly the number of those carrying coffins which passed us going upstream gives colour to the story. It was curious to see the boats being towed along by men walking beside them in the water harnessed as trackers. Lower down, the river becomes deeper, and some of the

OTTER FISHING ON MIN RIVER

1. POLICE BOATMAN: MIN RIVER

2. SIGNBOARD OF INN

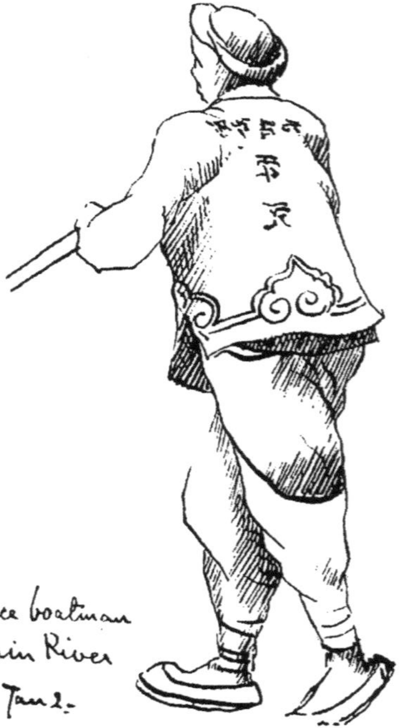

Police boatman
Min River
Jan 2-

Sign board of our
hotel at [illegible] Hsien

rapids look very pretty, as the water is a bluish-green colour and the rocks are red sandstone. Sometimes the road from the riverside leads up precipitous hills by long stone staircases. The reflections of the common blue clothes of the people, as seen in the river, are an exquisite turquoise colour. The scenery becomes increasingly beautiful as one proceeds down the river. Our escort was changed daily, and one man brought a fowling-piece on board with which to beguile the time. He tried to shoot the wild ducks, which are the size and colour of our tame ones, but he had not the smallest success. We were interested to see the loading of the weapon, which had a piece of smouldering rope finally thrust down the barrel, preparatory to its being fired off. The gun had to be balanced on a bundle of sticks while careful aim was taken at a very near bird sitting quite still. Even then, the bird was in no danger, so far as we could see, but ineffectual attempts to shoot kept the man busy all day. The soldier wore a silver ring, of which he was extremely proud. This had to be entrusted to the other soldier each time that he fired his weapon. Part of the way we had police boatmen, who spent some time in rowing, and were of material assistance to us; but unfortunately this was only a rare occurrence.

Kiating was the first large town we reached, and here we left the boat in order to make our expedition to Mount Omi.

CHAPTER XVII

Mount Omi

WE reached Kiating in the morning, and set to work at once on our preparations for the next day. The people there considered us very extraordinary for wishing to make the ascent at such an unusual time of year, and told us that it would be worse than useless, for we should certainly see nothing at all from the top. They pointed out how arduous an ascent it would be, as the snow would make climbing extremely difficult. The weather had been cloudy for some time, and we were in the land of mists, but nothing would deter us from our intention. We had read discouraging accounts of other travellers who had been up there, and it certainly sounded as if we should find the ascent beyond our strength, but we determined, at all events, to *try*. We arranged to take as little luggage as possible, but it was necessary to take food for six days, as on the sacred mountain there are no inns. There are plenty of monasteries, which give you reasonable accommodation, but it was quite unlikely we should get food there. The first day we travelled across the plain some twenty miles to the foot of the mountain. The scenery was pretty, but nothing remarkable was to be seen at this time of the year. One of the principal objects of interest is the white wax tree, a sort of ash, called by the Chinese "Pai-la-Shu." The white wax insects are bred in the celebrated valley of the Chien-ch'ang, some 200 miles away among the mountains. When they reach the right stage of development they are put in paper boxes, in bamboo trays, and brought to the plain of Kiating by the swiftest runners. These men only travel by night, as it is essential that the process of development should not proceed too rapidly. The boxes have to be opened every day and ventilated, and the men secure the best rooms in the inns, so that other travellers have much to suffer if they are on the road at the same time. Finally, the education of the grub is finished in the plain round Kiating.

We crossed a large river, and cliffs were pointed out to us containing caves called Man-tsi dwellings, and we were told that they were formerly inhabited by aborigines of that name. The banks of the Min River are honeycombed with them, and it is only quite recently that this Chinese tradition has been called in question. A resident in that district, who was interested in the pottery mounds left by the Man-tsi when they were driven farther west by the Chinese during the Han dynasty (200 B.C.–200 A.D.), was told of the existence of an earthenware coffin. He went to see it, and further investigation proved that such coffins were to be found habitually in the caves, together with fragments of household implements. He found also drawings of architectural columns and figures of winged gods and winged animals carved on the rock, of a totally different character from anything Chinese. The caves differ very much in size, varying from small ones, ten feet deep by seven broad and seven high, to large ones, a hundred feet in depth and eight or ten feet broad and seven or more high. Some of the larger ones have side compartments. Sometimes large simple caves are to be found some thirty or forty feet square, and they are supported by pillars of rock, with well-chiselled chapiters and ornamental masonry above them. These caves have all the same kind of doorways, but they vary considerably in fineness of design and execution. Some of the lintels and sides are well carved. The entrances have been built up, and sometimes so skilfully filled in with earth that all external traces of them are obliterated.

As may be supposed, a large number of these caves have been broken into by the Chinese and rifled of their contents. In a cave opened at Penshau in 1908, two skeletons were found lying on either side of the entrance, one with a long sword lying beside it, and the other with a short sword. There were small images in niches at the upper end of the cave, and a large jar full of cash, besides many household dishes. As this was evidently the burying-place of a poor family, there were no earthenware coffins; but in a similar one, evidently belonging to a rich family, the corpses were all in earthenware coffins, the material of which was the same as that now used in the district for making tiles for the houses. In this cave there were a number of birds and domestic animals in burnt clay, a variety of crockery, and various traces of its former wealth, but it had evidently been robbed of such things as the brass basins and cash which are found in these wealthier tombs. The writer of the article in the *North China Herald* (Dec. 26, 1908), from whose account I have made this brief summary, goes on to say that the coffins are made in two pieces, the main body and the lid. He investigated a large number of these caves, which are being ruthlessly destroyed by the natives, who have no idea of the value of what they find in them, and will sell such things as swords for a few pence to be used as old iron. Stone coffins are also not uncommon in them. The caves were evidently closed about the beginning of the Christian era, when the Man-tsi were still living on the banks of the Min River. It is to be hoped that some capable archæologist will soon take up the study of these caves before it is too late, as evidently there is much to be learnt with regard to the history of the Chinese as well as of the Man-tsi in that district.

Marco Polo, in referring to the Man-tsi district, mentions the widespread culture of cinnamon, and what we procured in Chengtu was certainly the most delicious we had ever tasted.

Rain began to fall as we neared the town of Omi, and we found there was no chance of our getting farther that night. Fresh coolies had to be engaged the next day, as it requires experienced men for going up the mountain. The usual method of being carried is to sit on a wooden perch attached to the shoulders of the coolies. A young American whom we met had been carried up to the top in this way. At one point the coolie stopped on the edge of a precipice to take a little rest, and suddenly stooped down, so that the American hung over the abyss. On his uttering a remonstrance, the coolie remarked quite unconcernedly, "Have no fear ; I am only picking up a pebble with my toes." He was standing on one leg !

We arranged to start at our usual hour, 6.30 ; but we waited for a long time in vain. A few coolies came and fussed round the luggage, but while the others were being brought they disappeared, so that we began to fear we should never do our stage. A great deal of scolding and losing of one's temper (no simulation in the present case, though that is often necessary in China in order to make the coolies start) had to be gone through before we started. At last we got off at 8 o'clock, with the understanding that the coolies were to get us as far as Wan Yen Sz that day, for we had been told that we must be sure to go to that place and stop at a comfortable monastery. There are seventy monasteries on the mountain ; some of them very large, but others small and ill-kept. As soon as we left the plain the scenery became more and more beautiful. At the foot of it magnificent banyans and groups of sacred cedars formed a fine contrast to the slender trunks of the other trees. Then we came to a charming crystal stream, shaded by

MOUNT OMI BRIDGE

arching bamboos. The path was so narrow that whenever we met any one, they had to stride across the stream to let us pass, or they would scuttle away (if they were women) to some spot where there was room to stand, for the chair-bearers never pause or give way to other passengers; they simply ignore their being there and walk straight into them. Maidenhair and every kind of lovely fern was reflected in the green water. As we went up the valley the path led perilously round lofty rocks; once my chair stuck fast, unable to be moved either way, with the horrible precipice yawning below. My bearers yelled (from anger, not fear, I think), and one of the soldiers happily came to the rescue, for I cannot think what would have happened otherwise. Another time one of the front coolies fell flat coming down a flight of steps, so that on the whole we found that part of the journey very anxious work, both going up and coming down. We soon abandoned our chairs and began walking up endless flights of steps. We crossed an interesting little bridge ornamented with a dragon facing up the stream, whose tail projected from the farther side of the bridge, as in the sketch. These dragons are a favourite ornament of bridges in this province, and are there not merely for ornament but also to ward off the evil spirits. That is why they always face up the stream. The person crossing the bridge is a typical Szechwan woman.

We reached Wan Yen Sz much earlier than we expected. The bronze elephant in the temple there is considered very interesting, but it is certainly not ornamental. It is said to have come from India, and how it was conveyed thence nobody can explain. It had been damaged by fire, and there was a large hole in the under side, so a shrine had been made there, and two little Buddhas put in it, with incense in front. The tail was also extremely defective, so bits of incense like hairs had been stuck at the end of it. The Chinese really have no sense of the ludicrous in such matters, though they have a keen sense of humour, and one is constantly tempted to laugh in the temples. Happily, they do not mind this at all, and would not think that we were showing any lack of reverence. In the adjoining temple the monks were chanting, while two or three of them kept up a continuous beating on the Buddha fish and other gongs, as seen in the sketch. In front of the Buddha, and almost concealing him, was a large stone monument put up by an Indian prince. Near here we were shown a piece of stone which was said to be the Buddha's tooth. It weighed several pounds, and is much venerated by pilgrims.

We provided ourselves with stout pilgrim staves, which we found of the utmost value on both our upward and downward journeys. They have quaintly carved dragons or tigers at the top, with a loose wooden pea which rattles in their mouths. These sticks cost from a penny to 2½d., and after the pilgrimage has been performed it is the correct thing to have them painted red and black and gold. The

1. BUDDHIST MONK BEATING FISH GONG WHILE CHANTING

2. TIGER SHRINE

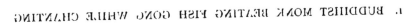

1. BUDDHIST MONK BEATING FISH GONG WHILE CHANTING

2. TIGER SHRINE

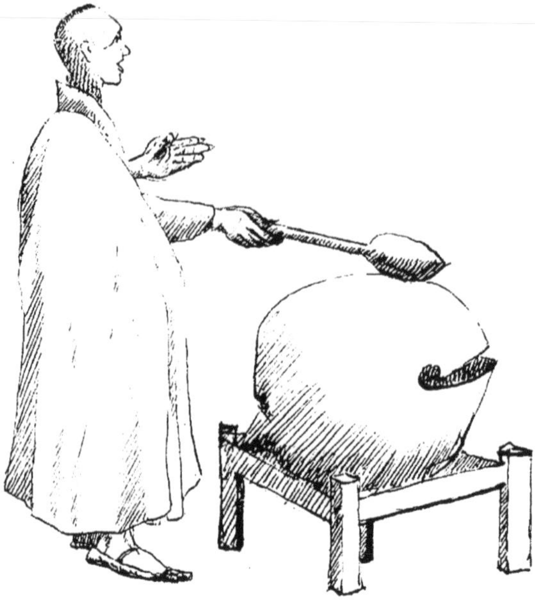

BUDDHIST MONK, CHANTING

tiger is the mountain god who was worshipped long before the existence of the Buddha, and whose shrines are still to be seen all the way up the mountain, with incense burning before them.

It was interesting to find on Mount Omi the two great Chinese symbols of power, the dragon and the tiger. As Laurence Binyon puts it: "In the superstitions of literal minds the Dragon was the genius of the element of water, producing clouds and mists; the Tiger the genius of the Mountains, whose roaring is heard in the wind that shakes the forest. But in the imagination of poets and of artists these symbols became charged with spiritual meanings, meanings which we should regard as fluid rather than fixed, and of imports varying with the dominant conceptions of particular epochs. In the Dragon is made visible the power of the spirit, the power of the infinite, the power of change; in the Tiger the power of material forces."

It is worthy of note that the Buddhists selected mountains already sacred, where they might establish themselves and form Buddhist sanctuaries. They tolerated the gods in possession, so that they still continue to be worshipped simultaneously with the Buddha. The mixing up of religions is seen everywhere in China, but nowhere did we notice it so grotesquely carried out as here. We counted no fewer than twelve tiger shrines on the way up the mountain, many of them with vivacious beasts half out of their shrines, as if they were tired of their rôle and were meditating a raid on their worshippers. In the evening the Abbot had prepared a feast for us, but we declined it, so he sent in a tray of nuts and sweets instead.

The following morning we set off betimes on foot, and very soon the coolies left the carrying-poles behind, and were obliged to carry our chairs on their backs. Soon the steps became almost continuous and increasingly slippery. The longest flight was over 1200 steps, and as the steps sloped downwards and were covered with ice the ascent was most fatiguing and toilsome. The day was grey and cloudy, but the shifting mists revealed crags and abysses, and all along our path there was a wealth of lovely shrubs—camellias, rhododendrons, bamboos, and ferns. The frost had coated everything, and the leaves were reproduced in ice, looking exactly like clear glass; sprays of dead blossom, tall grasses, delicate ferns, everything was duplicated in ice, and the slight thaw early in the day detached this ice from the vegetation. We were sorry not to see in full beauty the flowers and ferns for which Mount Omi is justly celebrated, but it would have been impossible to conceive anything lovelier than what we did see.

Our midday halt at a monastery was provokingly long, as the men's food had to be cooked, so that we did not start for a couple of hours. The sight of fowls here was a pleasant surprise to us, as the Buddhists obviously could have no use for them and our larder needed replenishing. We secured some eggs, and asked for a fowl also. When we came to pay for it, however, the monks said that they did not sell anything. If we liked to put our names down on their subscription list (which a monk forthwith produced) for the restoration of the monastery, we should be welcome to a fowl as a gift, not otherwise. We set out again, and found our way grow more and more precipitous and slippery. We met Tibetan pilgrims, a wild and fierce-looking company, toiling painfully upwards like ourselves, or slithering down. All these are welcomed and entertained in the monasteries. Our soldier escort was evidently very much afraid of them, and had a great deal to say of their evil doings, warning us to keep close together and close to himself. As I approached a group of pilgrims in one of the monasteries, in order to watch a man blowing up his fire with a goatskin bellows, one of them scowled at me and waved me away, as if he feared our sharing his thieving propensities. This is the season for Tibetan pilgrims, and many of them had travelled far, bringing their beasts of burden with them. The Chinese pilgrims come in the spring, and there was a big pilgrimage ten years ago—so a monk told us. The air grew intensely cold and dense, and, as twilight fell, our men urged us to halt about two miles short of the summit, where there was a good monastery. To this we willingly agreed, the more so as my breathing had grown extremely difficult, and I was beginning to feel at the end of my strength. Our lofty room was clean and well built, and the ten beds around it all stood empty. Soon a large glowing brazier was brought in, and we were thankful not only to get warm, but also to dry our clothes, which were heavy with mist.

Mount Omi is 11,000 feet high, and Kiating is only 1200, so we had come into a wholly different temperature, and when we woke in the morning it was to find everything frozen hard—sponges like boards, oranges as hard as bullets, and the water in my sketching-bottle a lump of ice. But the sun was shining brilliantly, and the mountain-top was a dazzling vision of loveliness emerging from a vast ocean of clouds. It took us about an hour to arrive at the summit, and the priest told us that as the sun shone we were evidently good people. This was highly satisfactory, as so many people thought us fools for attempting the ascent at this time of year, telling us of all the people who had toiled to the top and seen nothing. We anxiously inquired at what time of day we could see "Buddha's Glory," a sort of Brocken spectre which is rarely seen by travellers, and which we were told could not be seen at all at this time of year. Standing on the edge of the summit, you look down a precipice of more than a mile, and we could only feast our eyes on the ever-changing scene, the clouds looking as if they were boiling up from some hidden caldron, now concealing, now revealing the peaks of distant mountains. On a clear day the far-distant snowy peaks of Tibet are visible, and the glorious fertile plain out of which the limestone peak of Mount Omi rises.

SUMMIT OF MOUNT OMI

was highly
fools for
telling us
and seen
time of

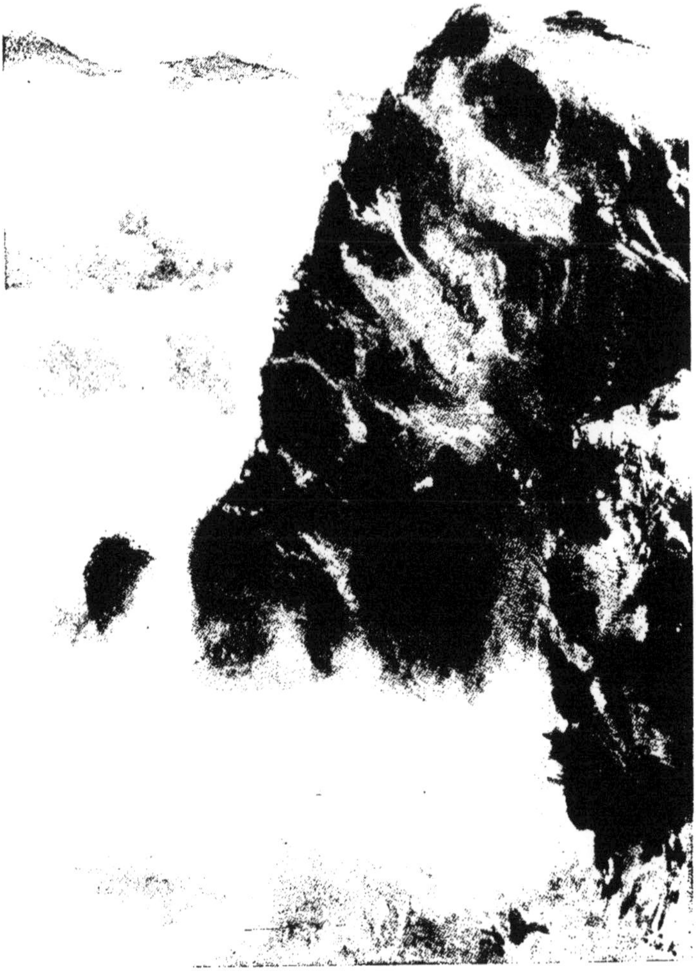

I established myself in a sunny nook under the temple eaves, and sent for hot water with which to sketch the neighbouring crag of the "10,000 Buddhas." After lunch I sketched the interior of the Buddha shrine with all its gaudy, squalid trappings, a harmony in reds. I was amazed to see the brevity of the worshippers' prayers; owing, I think, to their fear of my introducing them into the sketch. The three figures of the Buddha were behind a large red curtain, in which were openings through which they could be dimly discerned. We went back to our former quarters for the night, but had very little rest, as the coolies went in for a night of revelry, in which we felt sure the monks shared, although our suggestion to that effect next day was vehemently repudiated. The descent of the mountain we found extremely arduous, despite our being shod with straw sandals and having the support of our pilgrim sticks; it was dreadfully slippery, and for six and a half hours we toiled steadily down flights of steps, or glissaded down them on our backs. We calculated the distance as not much less than twelve miles. The stiffness produced was not quite so bad as I had anticipated, but it makes you feel extremely foolish to have to watch each step you take in order to be sure that your feet are obeying your bidding. Then you see the coolies pick up the chairs and carry you for another three hours after you are dead beat as if they had done nothing. We spent the night at a clean new inn about three miles from the town of Omi, and for the first time we occupied an upstairs bedroom in a Chinese house. After this occasion we always used to try and secure one, but our stiffness then made it extremely painful to get up the steep staircase. It was like mounting into a loft, and was a very pleasant variety from any inn we had yet encountered.

The following morning we made an early start, so as to have a little time in Kiating to collect our belongings and go on board a boat to take us to Sui Fu. Our temper was sorely tried by the delay of our men and the changing of some of them at Omi Hsien, which delayed us about an hour. By dint of offering extra pay, however, we made up some time, and came upon an interesting sight to beguile us on the way—namely, cormorants and an otter fishing. When we got to the Tong River—the third river that we saw at the base of the mountain—we were rowed down to Kiating, a distance of some four miles. We were curious to see what the coolies would pay for the boat journey, as they had arranged the matter. For the four chairs and the eighteen people, the whole cost was thirty cash—namely, three farthings. We got back to Kiating soon after four o'clock, and found that our friends had kindly got everything ready for our departure. The thought of two quiet days on the boat was not unacceptable after a somewhat laborious but entirely satisfactory trip up Mount Omi, and it was many days before we recovered from our stiffness. Owing to mist, we did not see the impressive view of Mount Omi as it rises from the plain.

CHAPTER XVIII

From Szechwan into Yünnan

THE boat in which we continued our journey down the Min River was rather larger than the one we had previously, but still we could not stand upright in it. It is not always easy to get just what you want in the way of boats, especially at this time of year; but it was not a long journey, although our men took about four times as long as they ought to have done, and it was only by offering extra payment that we managed to do it in two days. We had one piece of good luck on the way. Our kind friends at Chengtu, when replenishing our stores, had lamented the non-arrival of a large case of biscuits sent out by friends in England, mentioning the name of the firm from which they were coming. As we neared Sui Fu we were watching divers getting up cases which had evidently been shipwrecked, and conspicuous amongst them was a large case bearing the name referred to. On arrival at Sui Fu we reported this at the mission station where we stayed, and learnt that they had heard of the wreck and sent to inquire whether the case had been got up. Shortly afterwards their messenger returned, saying that it could not be found. Our information being explicit, we described exactly the spot where we had seen the wreck, a few miles above the town ; the man was sent again and told that he *must* bring the case, as we had seen for ourselves that it had been got up. This time he returned in triumph with it. Probably the divers thought that they would get a better price by selling the contents, and if we had not seen it our friends would not have seen it either.

The town of Sui Fu is most charmingly situated, lying at the junction of the Yangtze and the Min rivers, and is enclosed in a fork between the two, with beautiful hills rising above it. Its name is both spelt and pronounced in various ways, to the great bewilderment of those who address letters. It is Sui Fu, or Hsui Fu, or Sú Cheo, or Schow, or Su Chau, or it may be rendered in various other ways. Well might the London telegraph clerk say to my sister, "If you send a wire it is only at your own risk," in answer to my wire from Peking giving the Pekinese spelling. It is a busy and flourishing place, and possesses a Roman Catholic cathedral as well as a convent.

A Roman Catholic priest is deeply interested in the local divinity, which is certainly an interesting specimen of art, if nothing more ; but the priest is firmly persuaded that it is St. Thomas, and takes all his friends to see it. The god is enshrined in a temple on a hillside overlooking the town. It is a most beautiful situation, but somewhat spoilt by the fact that it is entirely covered with graves. Hills are frequently

COPPER IDOL, SUI FU

四川省敘府真武山大銅菩薩披髮祖師像

utilised for this purpose, and contain thousands of graves. The gaudily painted figure is 18 feet high and $5\frac{1}{2}$ feet broad, made of fine red copper. It stands on a large bronze turtle, from which, unfortunately, a good part has been stolen; the head alone is in excellent preservation. It was erected some hundreds of years ago by the Lolos or Ibien, an aboriginal tribe who then held possession of this part of the country. They believed that he was a saint who came over the seas on a turtle, and this certainly corresponds with the legend of St. Thomas going to India. It is a very truculent-looking saint, not lightly to be parted from his sword. The figure is well fenced off from view by large bars, though one has been removed, so that people can push through and get a closer look at him. While I was busy sketching, a priest came up to look, with his long hair fastened on the top of his head by a carved wooden pin. The priests do not plait their hair, but simply twist it up into a sort of "bun." A woman came up with offerings—fowl, sweets, &c.—which, after they had been offered to the god, she would take home and eat with the greater relish. This is certainly a way of killing two birds with one stone, as she was too poor to have eaten chicken on ordinary occasions. As we came down the hill we met the chief mourner of a funeral, wearing the coarsest sackcloth, which he could scarcely prevent from falling off, as it is incorrect on such occasions to gird it round the waist.

We left Sui Fu on January 14th, *en route* for Yünnan

Fu, and felt that the seasons had got strangely mixed up, as we wended our way along the banks of the Yangtze. This part of it is called the "river of the golden sand." It is quite a misnomer, for it is as mud-coloured as ever. The peas were in various stages of growth in the part of the river-bed from which the water had subsided. Some looked lovely with their white, pink, or plum-coloured blossoms; others were quite small, only a few inches high; and others again we enjoyed for our evening meal. The people were all busy harvesting the sugar-cane, and we seemed to be the only persons here not chewing it. Our soldiers surreptitiously stole it from the loads that were being carried along the road. Beautiful orange groves on the steep slopes above the river were full of ripe fruit. Men were busy preparing the soil for other crops by breaking the sods with mallets after they had been ploughed. The whole land is one great ceaseless field of labour, where every one works from early childhood to extreme old age.

On the fourth day's journey we reached the borders of the province of Yünnan. Our road parted from the Yangtze and ran for many days parallel with a lovely river (of a deep blue-green colour like those in the Pyrenees), whose course we followed from the point where it fell into the Yangtze up to its birthplace in the mountains. Sometimes the pathway winds high up the hill-sides, and sometimes almost down to the river's edge. The cormorants were busy fishing —not for John Chinaman, but for themselves. We

CORMORANTS THE CORMORANT RIVER

had the merriest set of sturdy carriers, who treated our weight as if it were a mere joke, and laughed and ran with us, despite the roughness of the way, and rather to our terror sometimes. They are much stronger than the ordinary Szechwan coolies. Indeed, that is a necessity in the case of these roads, which are no better than sheep-tracks in the Cumberland fells, despite their being the great trade-route between the two largest provinces of Western China. Day by day we revelled in the beauty of the scenery and its ever-varying charms. There was subtler charm in them than there would have been when the flowers are in blossom, for it was the moment when the earth was awakening after its winter sleep; every twig was beginning to change colour; the buds were swelling; the delicate fronds of innumerable ferns were uncurling; the birds were hesitatingly trying their notes; and the sun had not yet given the dazzling blue to the sky which comes later on. It only illuminated and irradiated, but did not dazzle the eyes. We felt that we had come exactly at the right moment, for the weather was perfect for walking, and it was not nearly so cold as we expected. The inns are not so bad as they have been described, and we came on one where there was a beautifül large window—above the pig-sty—overlooking the country, and the unwonted light had encouraged travellers to make remarks on the walls in French, German, and English, as well as Chinese.

After entering Yünnan we came to a substantial

suspension-bridge, made of eight parallel iron chains, and with chain hand-rails; but the planks on it were strewn about in a desultory way, calculated to upset unseasoned travellers. At either end of the bridge was a solid block of masonry, surmounted by a temple through which the chains passed and were buried deep into the ground. These bridges are often a considerable length, and do not hang at a natural swing, but are drawn up as tightly as possible with hawsers; which, of course, makes a heavy strain upon the chains. This kind of bridge is to be found throughout the province, and they always seem in good condition. We cannot help wishing that a little of the engineer's skill had also been expended on the steep rough track which led up from the bridge. The roads are apparently never mended, and in some places had fallen away, or had been covered by a small landslip.

It was curious to see the change of vegetation when we crossed the border, the poppy replacing the pea to a large extent. Yünnan is the greatest opium-growing province in the Empire, and the best; but there is already a perceptible diminution since the new anti-opium Acts. We saw peas of various kinds, and one that is grown for making oil is quite peculiar: the peas grow three together like a berry. As we approached a somewhat barren district the men had to have a feast at our expense, and in view of the future scarcity of their much-esteemed pork, our soldiers had provided themselves with a large joint, which I found in one of the coolies' hats attached to the back of my

LAOWATAN RIVER

chair. They never scrupled to hang their dainties, besides an extensive wardrobe, pipes, &c., on to our chairs, and as the day proceeded they peeled off their coats till they had shed three or four at the least.

We noticed an odd procession one day wending its way along the opposite river-bank. First came a white banner with apparently two mourners; then a few people carrying little pennons of various colours; then a pig borne aloft on a shutter; then more boys and men carrying pennons; the whole accompanied by the beating of drums. The procession was on its way to a grave to pay homage to a dead ancestor, in which ceremony the pig would be the *pièce de résistance* at a sort of perennial feast for the dead. Later on we met a procession carrying a corpse on a stretcher, with no signs of mourning beyond a man strewing paper money after it.

We followed the beautiful river Laowat'an as far as the village of that name, and up to this point we were continually accompanied by the unmelodious cries of trackers pulling large junks up the rapids; beyond that point navigation is impossible. Laowat'an means "Cormorant rapid," and although it is quite a good-sized village, we found that the only room at the inn was very small, filled with four dirty beds, with no window, and close to the most noxious open drain. Having seen in Little's pamphlet about this journey that he had stayed at a native evangelist's house here, we took the hint and sent to see if we could do likewise. We received an answer in the affirmative, and found that the house was close by. Though the evangelist himself was not at home, we were warmly welcomed by his wife. She took us to a nice large upper room, with a most attractive window overlooking the street, which was full of an amusing crowd busy marketing. One man's occupation appeared to be carrying a pipe round, from which people had a whiff or two. We found our new quarters vastly more entertaining than the inn, and held an interesting conversation with our hostess by means of pictures and dumb-show, as we had no one to interpret. I hope we did not tell many lies by mistake, but fear that it is not improbable. The next morning we felt quite sorry to leave these nice people, who had been so friendly to us. We were greatly struck with the fine poultry all through this district. My Aberdonian poulterer would with great justice describe them as "some fine beasts." There are the handsomest pure white and coal-black hens, besides fowls of various colours. The eggs, too, are a splendid size, and are to be obtained everywhere. The peculiarity of the fowls is that many of them have black skins and black bones, which are most unappetising to look at, but they are considered the best kind for eating. There were plenty of vegetables, pears, oranges, and peanuts to be had, and so far we could see no signs of the dearth of food of which we had heard such alarming accounts. There are everywhere pigs in abundance: some of them are a curious fawn colour.

1. OUR MILITARY ESCORT

2. "ORPHAN SPIRIT" SHRINE

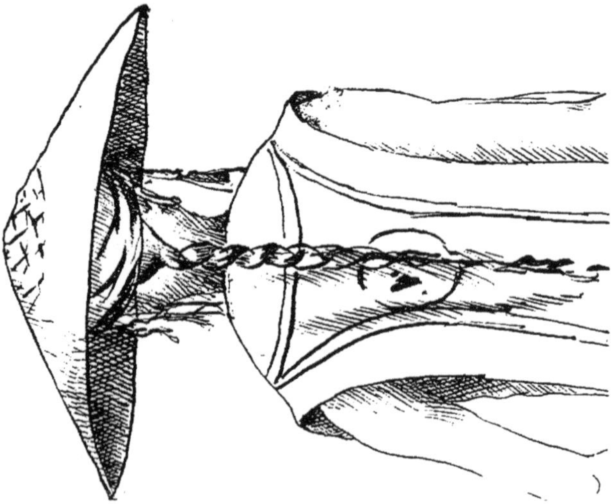

We crossed a fine suspension-bridge after leaving Laowat'an, and took a path leading upwards for about a couple of hours over the mountains. A light for the "orphan spirits" might well be needed on such a road. The chair-carriers found it difficult work, and we got on much more quickly on our own feet; though the coolies made no suggestion that we should walk, despite the fact that we had authorised them to do so whenever the road was difficult. They are so willing and attentive in performing any little service—such as cleaning one's boots after walking through a quagmire—that one the more gladly saves them when the road is stiff. One coolie fell and wrenched his knee rather badly, but he went on most uncomplainingly, and showed intense gratitude on getting it bathed and bandaged. In fact, from this time on he was our devoted slave. We were interested to meet quite a new god in this region. He has three faces, and often wears a large stone hat. He is carved in stone, and stands by the roadside like a little milestone at intervals all along the way; but frequently there are no signs of worship about him. He is called by the Buddhist formula "O mi to fu," and is worshipped by the coolies to prevent their getting sore feet, so they frequently burn sandals (quite new ones) before him, and incense sticks may be seen in front of his image. Day by day we went up and down the most precipitous places, gradually rising to the Yünnan plateau. The road grew worse and worse, being much injured by the long trains of pack-animals. Ponies, mules, and donkeys are driven in parties of from ten to thirty ; and not only do they make the road full of little round holes, but also they are a dreadful hindrance, frequently completely blocking the way. The path, besides, has large round stones embedded in it, which are polished by the coolies' sandals till they shine like porphyry. One day we met dozens of mules going down a breakneck zigzag staircase in the rocks, and we were bespattered by them with mud from head to toe, being compelled to wait while they went past. How they keep their footing it is hard to tell, and it is sad to see their sore backs when their loads are off. The loads being carried are of a most varied description : copper, tin, coal, salt, skins, spices, chillies, armadillo skins, paper, bowls, opium, and later in the season large quantities of the wax insect "larvæ." In a recent official report the road from Sui Fu to Chaotung is described as one of the worst in the Empire, but it is good compared with others in the north of the same province. The Chinese have given picturesque names to some of these bad ones, such as "The King of Hell's Slide," the "Gate to Hell," the "Last Look at Home," the "Place where the Soul is Lost." Describing this road on the borders of Babuland, where the Lolos live, S. Pollard writes that from one spot he counted no fewer than sixty towers of refuge.

For ten days we followed the course of the Laowat'an, or Taquan River, till at last we traced it to its source where it gushes out of a hole from the bowels of the mountain as quite a large, brawling

1. TOWER OF REFUGE

2. "OMI TO FU" SHRINE

1. TOWER OF REFUGE

2. "OMI TO FU" SHRINE

3-faced
"O mi to fu" with
coolies' sandals burnt
before it to prevent
sore feet on a journey
Yunnan province.

stream in a sort of cul-de-sac of the hill. Its banks are frequented by the ubiquitous wagtail, the fierce-eyed cormorant, and the most cheery little blackbird with a white cap and black-tipped chestnut tail, which it flirts as assiduously as the water wagtail does. In one part there was a fine limestone crag overshadowing the river, and high up in its ledges there are still to be seen dilapidated fragments of coffins, said to date back as far as the time of the Ming dynasty. How they were conveyed to such a position it is difficult to conceive. For an hour after leaving the stream we climbed laboriously up the hillside till we were swallowed in the mist, and at last emerged into quite a different and much more familiar landscape, a bog moorland, on which were scattered thatched cottages from which a pleasant smell of burning peat greeted our nostrils. We felt as if we were suddenly transported to Ireland. We sat down to rest by a cottage where a woman was selling inviting-looking sweets, and she was as pleased as our men were when we distributed them among the party. They were made of the nuts and sugar grown in the neighbourhood. Not an hour before, we had left groups of bamboos and tall fan palms, and the contrast of the new country was certainly very startling. The cottagers looked poor and scantily clad, and from this point on they seemed to be poorer and poorer looking.

All the next day we gradually descended towards the city of Chaotung, and it appeared to be a specially auspicious day for pig-killing (the people are very particular in such matters), in preparation for their New Year festivities. Every house almost that we passed that morning was the scene of these preparations, and the keenest interest and expectation was depicted on every face but our own. Our coolies would have dearly loved to stop to watch the entertainment, but, as may be supposed, we did not allow this.

The prefectural town of Chaotung was reached after passing through a dull plain, across which a piercing wind was blowing, which is characteristic of this district. It is an interesting little place, and is much frequented by many of the Miao (aboriginal tribes) in their picturesque dress. The Wha Miaos (=flowery Miao) are so called because of the colour of their dress, which is dyed blue and red by an ingenious method of stencilling the cloth, using beeswax to make the design. They are totally unlike the Chinese, the only point of similarity being the wearing of the pigtail by the men; but they have a religion and language of their own, and keep absolutely aloof from the Chinese. The women, when married, wear their hair erected into a horn, which sticks out from the side of the head; but as soon as they have children the horn is erected straight up from the top. They are very shy people, but as I was anxious to get a sketch of a woman, I got the missionary to persuade her to sing while I made a few notes. She was dressed in a pretty red and blue garment, with a large felt cape

MIAO

OAIM AHW

MIAO WOMAN

Wha

over it, and wore a full short petticoat of blue and white. Both men and women wear gaiters and loose leather boots, and the men's sleeves are looped up in a picturesque way as in the accompanying sketch. The women carry their babies slung on their backs.

CHAPTER XIX

The Road to Yünnan Fu

AFTER a couple of days' halt we started for the capital, with new coolies for the most part—fine, strong men—who had arranged to do the twelve days' stages at four taels per man, with the additional inducement of a pork-feast on New Year's Day. The first day we passed through somewhat uninteresting country, but then we climbed up amongst the mountains and reached one specially fine point of view, from which we saw five ranges, one beyond the other, and to the west a lovely snow range. From there we made our way down a most precipitous slope to the bottom of a valley, where a noisy brook was spanned by one of the fascinating iron suspension-bridges. This bridge is composed of eight parallel thick iron chains with connecting links, and the masonry at each end is very fine. The hand-rails were decorated with graphic carvings of monkeys and other apocryphal beasts at each end. The little village was eminently picturesque, and the willows were already in their delicate spring green, contrasting well with the stiff blue-green prickly pears. Coming down the slope, our eyes had feasted on the sight of pink fruit blossom, and on the farther side of the stream we

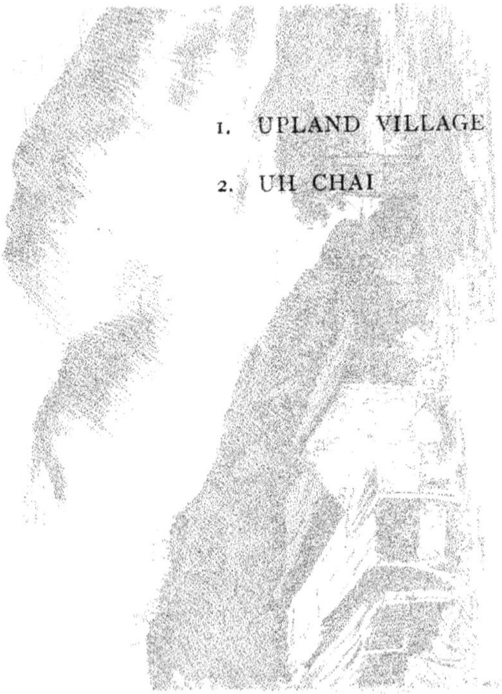

1. UPLAND VILLAGE

2. UH CHAI

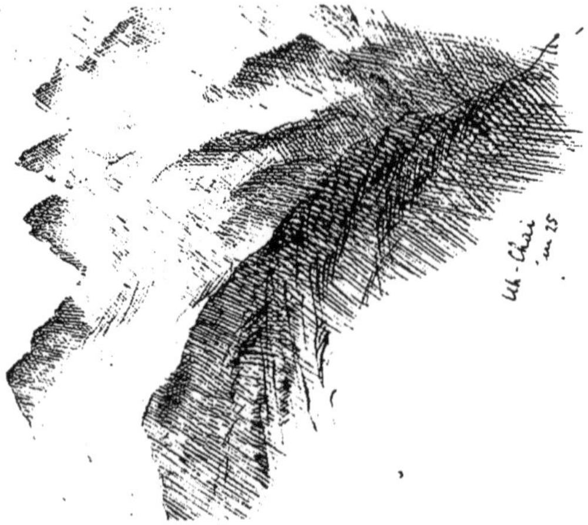

came next day to dazzling white pear-trees. Certain shrubs blossom even while snow is on the ground, and this is a favourite *motif* both in Chinese and in Japanese art.

All the trees were beginning to bud, and the birds to sing and mate, although it was only the end of January. As we neared Tungchwan Yun we saw various new species of birds, and especially large numbers of cranes, mainly grey, but some white, and one solitary black one standing alone on the edge of the stream, as their habit is. The first view of the city is picturesque, as it is seen from the high hills overlooking the plain full of rice-fields. The city nestles under the farther hill-side and looks as if it could be reached in an hour or so, whereas it takes at least three times as long. In a village at the foot of the hill the preparations for the New Year were in full swing. Every door was being cleaned for the new gods to be pasted up together with mottoes and other decorations. Great washing was going on in a large puddle in the middle of the village; clothes, bowls, cooking utensils, fowls for the feast, vegetables, &c. Close by were large flocks of wild ducks, teal, and other birds, which made one's mouth water to see, now that we had reached a part of the country where the residents can rarely get anything except pork and fowls in the way of meat. Tungchwan is quite pretty, owing both to its situation and to the number of trees in it. Also it looked remarkably clean and bright with its decorations, red, orange, blue, and gold, on all the doors ; but that may have been merely because it was New Year's Eve (January 31st). There was much less noise of crackers all night than we had expected, and we were told that the custom of keeping New Year's Day is much less formally observed than it used to be. Nothing would have induced our coolies, however, to travel that day, and all the shops were closed, and people were walking about in their new clothes and cleanly shaven. We went to see a Confucian temple on the outskirts of the town, which had evidently been visited by the scholars of the place, and in which there were little heaps of offerings, each consisting of five oranges in front of every tablet. There were a number of courtyards and some fine trees in them, especially some interesting specimens of the sensitive tree.—If you scratch the trunk every twig quivers. There are a great many insect trees throughout the whole district, in which the white wax insect is bred. Before they come out of the trunk little bunches of straw about the size of two fingers are tied to it, in which the larvæ are afterwards found. We were very sorry that lack of time prevented our making an excursion into the neighbouring district, which is inhabited by aboriginal tribes. The Wesleyan missionaries have been civilising some of these people, and one of their number has successfully reduced the Miao language to writing by an ingenious adaptation of Pitman's shorthand system. The tribesmen are able to read and write in a few weeks, and have taken to writing letters to one another like ducks to water. There are

1. YUNNAN HAT

2. LOLO WOMAN

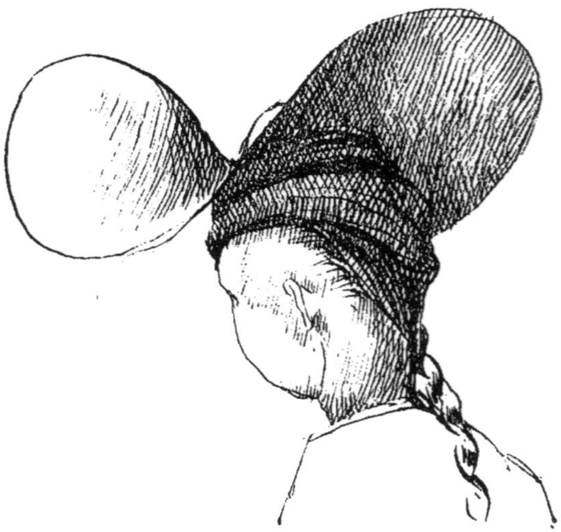

Yünnan hat

bien woman = i-lo.
Tong Chuan.

many different tribes among the mountains, some very shy and unapproachable, and with curious customs of their own. A member of the mission described to us a curious race that takes place in Bábú land where the Manzas live, but which had never been visited before by European women. The course is strewn with the feathers of fowls, and the men wear very full, short, circular dark capes, and a sort of crest on their heads. Then they put their ponies at full gallop, and extend their arms so that they look like eagles with extended wings as they sweep round the course *ventre à terre*, enveloped in a cloud of feathers and dust. Some of the tribes are very wild ; not infrequently the Lolos or Ibien, as they prefer to be called, kidnap the Chinese and make them pay a heavy ransom, so that little towers of refuge are built in this district. The number of these aboriginal tribes is probably unknown to any one; we always heard conflicting accounts of them, and until recently no systematic attempt has been made to approach them. Hosie describes how difficult it was even to catch a glimpse of any of them when they were close beside the road, as they lurk in the bushes to try and see others, themselves unseen.

When we left Tungchwan the following morning we passed a temple at the entrance of which the tutelary gods and horses, larger than life-size, stand on either side in heavily barred halls, looking most ferocious. The gentry of the place have recently erected a new temple to the God of Riches, which we only saw from a distance. This has been done by means of a lottery, and perhaps the choice of a god is due to the great poverty of the district, where the people are always on the verge of starvation, and where a poor harvest means utter ruin to a large number. The result of this state of things shows itself in a repulsive way, for infanticide is extremely prevalent. In one hamlet near which we passed no fewer than thirty-three baby girls were thrown out recently in a single year; though it looked such a small place that I should not have imagined so many babies had been born in it altogether in the time. We were told that it was by no means uncommon to see such babies lying in the fields, and we were dreadfully exercised to know what we should do if we found one alive. Happily, our sense of humanity was not put to the test. We travelled through a long valley all day under a very hot sun, and longed for thinner clothing.

Next day we climbed the greater part of the way up precipitous hills in a cold, wet mist, longing for warmer winter clothes. Soon our hair was white like the bushes with rime, and we were truly thankful to be saved from the piercing wind which is usually found on these particular heights. The coolies are extremely superstitious about this wind, and would not dare to say anything in the way of complaint for fear the spirits should hear, even if it blew a hurricane. They are often obliged to turn round and wait till the fierce blasts are over; so they told us. The ice was so thick on our hair that we had to take it down before we could get it free from ice, and

1. BRIDEGROOM

2. FUNERAL PAGODA

our clothes were thoroughly wetted with it. For a couple of days the cold continued somewhat severe; then we got into the hot sunshine again, and even with a wind to refresh us we found travelling too hot. The hedges reminded one more of home, and there was a flowering tree not unlike hawthorn; also the hedges were full of cotoneaster, rose-bushes, and clematis.

The last three days of the journey to the capital are comparatively uninteresting across the plain, but we saw a quaint wedding journey as we left the hill country. First came four musicians, making a noise extremely like a bad performance on the pipes. Next rode the bridegroom, heavily adorned with scarlet and pink rosettes and sashes; his pony also decorated with scarlet, followed by a couple of men riding. Then came the scarlet wedding sedan-chair, sadly dilapidated by age and neglect, conveying the bride. She was followed by a finely dressed woman, riding, and one or two other people. Lastly came the bride's furniture—a very meagre supply of two chests and small boxes. We reached her destination before she did, and found the village awaiting her. In the street was a table spread as an altar, on which were two vases full of wild camellias, a vase of incense, and a tray containing three bowls of rice, one bowl of pork, with chopsticks standing erect in it, and two small bowls of spirit. In front of the table was a mat for prostration, and at each side of the street a bench with a red mat over it. When the cortège arrived we were among the onlookers, which seemed by no means acceptable to the people. After waiting for a few minutes and exchanging greetings, the whole party retired into the house, the bride being most carefully lifted out of her chair in as secret a manner as possible. We were much disappointed to see nothing of the ceremony, but Mr. Ku told us that evidently they had no intention of doing anything whilst strangers were looking on, so we had reluctantly to withdraw. As we heard that the wedding lasts three days, and that the guests are expected to sit and talk and eat each day from about 10 A.M. to 6 P.M., we comforted ourselves with the thought that it was better to see nothing than to endure that, and went away to our two-storied inn (the second that we have met), where we inhabited the attic with the fowls. This inn was so costly that our coolies had to go elsewhere, as we paid the exorbitant price of 2½d. each for board, bed, and bedding. Needless to say, the first and last items were of no use to us.

In one village we saw an interesting tall paper pagoda meant to be burnt at a funeral. It was painted mainly red. Throughout the empire it is customary to see extraordinary paper horses, servants, &c., as part of the requisites for a rich person's funeral. They are burnt at the grave, and are supposed to go to the other world with the spirit of the deceased, for his use. It is only rich people, who possess horses, servants, &c., for whom they are provided. As white is the colour of mourning in China, these models are made of white paper on light bamboo frames. Not infrequently I have seen a white cock in a basket on a coffin that is being taken to the grave, as the white cock is called a "spiritual" or "divine" fowl and is supposed to guide the spirit of the dead. These customs are already being superseded amongst the educated Chinese, and they are following our European plan of having flowers at funerals.

In the Viceroy Chang Chih-Tung's interesting book, "China's Only Hope," he arrives at a curious conclusion upon this point. He says: "Although they [Europeans] have no such things as ancestral halls and tablets of deceased relatives, in lieu of these they place the photographs of their dead parents and brothers [note the absence of sisters !] on the tables in their houses and make offerings of them. And while they make no sacrifices at the tombs of their ancestors, they repair their graves and plant flowers upon them as an act of worship."

Ancestral worship is so much the most important part of religion in China, that the foregoing account of our habits is meant to dispel an injurious prejudice against us.

There was one compensation in leaving the mountains and crossing the hot and dusty plain: the larks were singing as blithely as in England, the cranes were thoroughly busy over their livelihood, and squirrels were frisking in the trees. Villages are far more plentiful, and there is much more traffic on the road as the capital is approached. There are large fields of beans, and they are the sweetest-scented harvest there is, to my thinking.

The day we reached Yünnan Fu was one long aggravation, as the head coolie had made up his mind that we should not arrive that day, declaring that one hundred li (about twenty-six miles) was too far. We also had made up our minds that we *should* arrive, so we started an hour earlier, or, more correctly speaking, we got up an hour earlier. For the first time our men kept us waiting, and when at last they were ready to start they crept like snails. In vain we urged them on and held out promises of a pork feast in the evening. They stopped perpetually, and out of the first seven hours of the day they spent two hours resting. Finally, they were told that if they did not go on immediately and quickly they would forfeit the feast entirely, and then they almost ran, saying that the city gate would be shut. We thought that this was their usual excuse, but as we neared the walls in the fast-closing twilight a gun sounded which filled us with misgivings. My friend's chair had gone in front, contrary to our usual custom, as she was much the lighter load, and her coolies were apt to run away with her! When she reached the gateway she was in time to see the big gates slowly swing to, and to hear the bolt shut, after which the keys are at once carried to the magistrate's office. By the time we had all arrived we found that it would be possible to have the gates reopened by sending in a visiting-card to the magistrate along with our military escort. The power of a visiting-card is very great in China, and we had the satisfaction of winning the day after a great twelve hours' tussle with our men. It would be hard to say whether an Englishman or a Chinaman is the keener to get his own way!

CHAPTER XX

Yünnan Fu

THE approach to Yünnan Fu is really lovely, and pagodas and tall temples surmounting the walls give it an imposing air. It is much the most important city in the province, and is following hard in the wake of Chengtu in the matter of progress. As regards improvements, new schools, barracks, a mint, and a railway station have sprung up within the last few years, not to mention street lamps and foreign-looking police, a French hospital and a French post-office. The French have been gradually pushing their way here, but not altogether successfully. The railway station exists, but no railway. According to the contract it ought to have been already completed, but owing to the extreme unhealthiness of the districts through which it passes a great many of the engineers have either died or been incapacitated for work, so that the railway is not likely to be completed for several years to come. In fact, they can only work on it at certain times of the year, in consequence of malaria. The French post-office also exists, but has been shut by order of the authorities, and the relations between French and Chinese authorities are decidedly strained. The presence of the French in the city has sent up the price of everything. In fact, many ordinary commodities are double the price they were a few years ago.

We were much disappointed to find nearly all the shops closed, owing to its being the Chinese New Year, but we managed to find a few small things of interest to buy. What particularly charmed us was a set of painted scrolls. There was a whole series of different designs of birds, some of them beautifully coloured, which we bought for the modest sum of 10s. for the set of eight. Throughout China scrolls are hung on the walls for decorative purposes as we use pictures, and sometimes you find quite charming designs either hung up or painted on the walls of unpretentious inns. When we were in the main street standing chatting together at a short distance from our host, who was making a bargain for us, a woman came along and eyed us up and down attentively. She then began to speak to us, and although we did not understand anything she said, the subject was very obvious, as she pointed at her own waist (or rather the place where it should be visible) and then at ours, after which she made a small circle with her fingers and said, pointing at us, "Very pretty." Who would have dreamt that such a thing could have happened in China, where a visible waist is considered so extremely improper!

We found the most amusing time to be in the streets, however, was in the evening, when there were nightly exhibitions of Chinese lanterns, as ingenious as they are effective. A tiny lady's shoe made of coloured paper, with half an egg-shell for the heel and a few drops of oil to hold the floating wick in it, makes a charming little lantern. Large fishes with movable heads and tails look extremely pretty, and grotesque lions are made to promenade above the heads of passengers with life-like palpitations. Their eyes are also made of egg-shells, which were effectively used in many other lanterns also. Some of the more elaborate lanterns were hung outside the shops; others were for sale. For a few "cash" you can get little toy theatres, within which the warmth of the candle sets in motion revolving figures whose shadows are thrown on the front of the stage. There was an infinite variety of lanterns exhibited, and we much regretted that they were too flimsy to carry home; for they are all made on the lightest bamboo frames with thin coloured paper. Later on we saw the most interesting of all the lanterns, a large dragon which is many yards in length and of which the sections are carried by men; but as there had been considerable disturbances lately when this had been carried about the city, the authorities refused to allow it for the time being. It is at the time when people are holiday-making that they seem difficult to manage, but their vices are not such as to make them troublesome to travellers. Opium-smoking and gambling are certainly the worst of these vices, and they are the curse of this place.

TEMPLE OF THE GOD OF LITERATURE

Yünnan is surrounded by pretty places for excursions, so we set off one fine morning in our chairs to visit a metal temple about five miles distant, called "Gin Tien"—namely, "Golden Temple." As we passed through the sweet-scented bean-fields we saw many children enjoying swings, a sight we had not met before in any other part of the country. Soon we reached the foot of the hills and ascended through woods filled with a delicious aromatic scent; but the trees were quite unfamiliar to us, and whether it was from them or the brushwood that the scent came we could not determine. The temple was beautifully situated on the hillside, and the courts rose one above the other, with long flights of steps leading from one to another. At the top of the first flight was an archway surmounted by a temple containing a small wooden "god of literature." The design on the cover of "The Face of China" is the god of literature: in one hand he holds the brush and in the other a tablet, and he stands on one foot on a fish. Doolittle explains it thus: "There are two stars which the Chinese profess to have discovered to have the supervision of the affairs of this world relating to 'literature and the pencil.' One of these, Kue Sing, is said to be the fifteenth star of the twenty-eighth constellation, answering to parts of Andromeda and Pisces."

A miscellaneous collection of gods lined the sides of the court in open corridors, but they were much neglected and in a ruinous-looking condition. At the top of the steps was a terrace on which was a fine camellia tree in full bloom, and other shrubs, while chattering groups of white-and-black starlings lent animation to the scene. Another flight of steps led to a court in which was the fine copper temple, painted black and gold, standing on a platform made of the celebrated Tali marble. A metal flag and bells that tinkled in the wind hung from an adjoining flag-staff, and another camellia tree was a sheet of pink blossom standing in glorious contrast behind the temple close to a gateway. This gateway led into another courtyard, where there were rooms which could be hired by any one who wishes to spend a few days there. Europeans often make use of these hill temples in the hot weather, even inhabiting sometimes the same rooms as the gods, of whom a new use is made as pegs on which to hang clothes in lieu of wardrobes—a proceeding which in nowise shocks the Chinese worshippers.

We were by no means the only visitors to the temples. There was quite an array of chairs waiting in the courtyards. Some of the people were gambling, others having their midday meal, others lying on couches smoking opium or admiring the view; but of worship there was no sign whatever. While I sketched some women came to look on, and had a little conversation (strictly limited, owing to my ignorance). They carried beautiful orchids which they said they had gathered in the mountains. In fact, Gin Tien is to Yünnan Fu what Richmond is to London.

Another interesting excursion which we made was

to the Rock Temples above the lake of Yünnan. There is a canal, about two miles long, leading directly from the city to the lake, and our host sent to hire a boat the day previous to our excursion. The arrangement made was that we were to have a crew of four men, in order to convey us as rapidly as possible to our destination; but when we got on board we found that our four men were represented by a woman and her three boys, aged approximately sixteen, ten, and three. We remonstrated, but it was so comic that we could do nothing but laugh; and finally she hired a man to come and row, paying him about twopence a day, whereas we paid her five shillings. Arrived at the farther side, we had a steep climb through pine woods to the temples, which are impartially Buddhist and Taoist. They must have been hewn out of the cliffs with an immense amount of labour and cost, for the approach to the upper ones was through winding galleries cut in the solid rock. The gods themselves are in shrines cut in the rock, and at the top of all is a little temple dedicated to the "god of literature," which was also carved out of stone; and there were other gods carved above the entrance. From the little platform in front of it there is a marvellous view of the lake and plain stretched far below, where fishing-boats looked like insects, and over which floated the shadows of the clouds.

On our way down our servant had prepared tea at a Buddhist temple, where we sat on stools (on a platform) at a low table. At an adjoining table there was a large family party of men and boys also having a meal, the ladies and girls of the family taking theirs in an inner room. We could not help admiring the charming sets of baskets in which they had brought their provisions, and we found them very friendly and talkative. They had many questions to ask of us, and informed us that they were jewellers in the city, finally suggesting that we should all go home together! We felt that this would be far too slow a process when we saw the ladies with their tiny feet laboriously toiling downwards, with the help of walking-sticks to steady them. So we made our excuses and hastened back, as the sun was already getting low.

We dedicated our last day at Yünnan to shopping, for the shops were beginning to reopen after their long inaction for the New Year. This place was in former times a happy hunting-ground for bronzes, but there are not many to be had now, and none of any value, while all the prices have gone up, many of them a hundred per cent. Copper work is the special industry of Yünnan, though all the copper is supposed to go direct to Peking. There are two families who for many generations have had the monopoly of making beautiful little copper boxes inlaid with silver. The work is very fine, and some of the designs are particularly attractive. Skin boxes are a speciality of this place, and we found it necessary to get some in which to carry our purchases; we also added a coolie to our party, as the loads carried here are not allowed to exceed eighty pounds per man. If we could fly, how quickly should we reach Bhamo!—only 360 miles through the air, instead of 967 miles by the road, with a total ascent of 26,000 feet. This is a computation in Hosie's book, "Three Years in Western China," but I think the distances are decidedly overestimated. When we left Yünnan Fu our party numbered twenty-four, and our chairs looked much more dignified than on arrival. The poles were all carefully bandaged with bright-blue cotton like a mandarin's chair, because of the winds, as our head coolie informed us that otherwise the poles were apt to crack. We were told to expect high winds all the rest of our journey through this province, for they are prevalent at this time of year. The prospect sounded discouraging, for the sun was hot, and we were obliged to wear large hoods, as the sun and the wind together had nearly skinned our faces. However, like all our previous information about the journey, the difficulties proved much less serious than we expected. In fact, so far we had had nothing to complain of beyond the inevitable disagreeables one encounters on travelling away from the beaten track. As we left the city we noticed a curious mingling of the past and present at the city gate: on the one side a dismantled cannon made by, or under the direction of, the French Jesuit Fathers, and stamped with the Christian symbol; on the other side of the gate, a notice-board warning passengers to keep to the right side of the road.

Leaving the city, we soon reached the mountains,

and day by day skirted the upper part of them ; sometimes plunging down deep into the valleys, especially for our resting-places at night. The people seem a sturdy, solid race, but through the greater part of the province which we have traversed, and especially round the capital, they are greatly disfigured by goitre. Every day we see scores of people (even quite young children) suffering from this disease. The women do a large share of all the hard work, carrying heavy loads, despite their small feet ; the loads are fastened on by broad bands passed round the forehead, like those of Newhaven fishwives. These bands are frequently run through holes in a big wooden collar worn both by men and women. Some of these collars have pretty little bits of carving on them.

On the roads we met innumerable droves of pack-animals, mostly laden with blocks of salt. The pack-men have special inns where they put up, which are nothing more than stables, and scores of animals can be accommodated in them. Despite the badness of the roads and the rough way in which they are hustled along, we have not seen a single beast with broken knees. They are allowed to rest free from loads or saddles at midday, and to roll in the dust at pleasure. The loads are fastened on to a framework which fits into the saddle and so avoids the necessity of being adjusted on the animal itself. There are regular camping grounds for the pack-animals all along the road, and they seem the best tempered beasts imaginable. The leaders usually wear bright red rosettes

FELLOW-TRAVELLERS

on their heads, often with mirrors in them, and also the Government loads have brilliant flags attached, which give them a picturesque look. Some of them wear the long tails of the Amherst pheasant fastened between their ears, and look as proud of themselves as a fashionable London lady with the huge plumes now in fashion. Some of them wear bells, which are necessary so as to herald their approach on these narrow, winding, and precipitous highways.

Every day we were more enchanted with the beauty of the country and the delights of spring. The banks are carpeted with primulas, and the hill slopes bright with rose-coloured camellias, scarlet azalea, white and crimson rhododendrons, yellow jessamine, clematis, begonias, and numberless flowering shrubs, many of which we have never seen before. This is the part of the world from which the majority of our flowering shrubs have originally come. It would be a paradise for botanists, and makes one long for more knowledge of many subjects, so as to be able to enjoy the journey still more and profit by it more thoroughly.

The second day after leaving Yünnan Fu, there was an earthquake, and it is a mystery why the front of our room did not entirely collapse. The inns here are really superior, but on this occasion the outer wall of our room happened to be constructed in sections at all sorts of angles, none of them what they were meant to be, and with extensive gaps between. It was quite impossible to shut the doors, and there was no pretence of a fastening, so we had put up a curtain in order to obtain a small measure of privacy. Happily, the people did not seem so inquisitive as they used to be when I was travelling in China fifteen years ago. In fact, we rarely see eyes peering through holes in the paper windows. Glass windows are still unknown in the inns, except in an occasional one in Shantung.

At Lu Feng Hsien we had an amusing experience. As we were resting after our evening meal there was suddenly a great noise of drums, and we were told that the dragon lantern was in the street. It turned out to be a sort of entertainment given by a cash shop next door, and not only was there a very bedraggled-looking dragon about twenty feet long, but also fish lanterns and sundry fireworks. The men carrying the sections of the dragon leapt about like demons as the shower of "golden rain" (fireworks) was turned full upon them, and the dragon writhed with unwonted energy. The drums never ceased for a moment, so that it was rather a relief when the show came to an end by the exhaustion of the internal illumination of the dragon. We were stopping at an inn just outside the city wall, and when we left the next morning we crossed a fine suspension-bridge with an imposing archway at each end of it. The chief magistrate of the district happened to be travelling on the same road with us, and sent word ahead that we were to be accommodated in a charming inn that day, having invited us to stop at his Yamen in the city the previous night. When magistrates are travelling they always send to engage an inn

TOMB OF A PHILOSOPHER AMONG RICE-FIELDS

beforehand, and a little official flag is then hung outside to show that the inn is full. Mr. Ku suggested that we should go in for an official flag, but we feared lest complications should arise.

The fresh New Year mottoes put up on the doorposts of our room stated encouragingly that "all cultured people inhabit this room," and "the courtyard is full of chairs and carts," but, true to Chinese incongruity, our coolies filled one of the rooms and the pigs occupied the background!

Day after day new flowers and birds appear on our pathway—white camellias, daphne, dog-roses, a flight of brilliant green parrots, long-tailed tits, seagulls; though what they are doing out here we cannot imagine. At one village where we spent a night the magistrate sent word that the people were in a somewhat disturbed condition, so he would send a special watch to guard us. We strolled out into the fields to try and get a sketch of the large flocks of cranes feeding in the rice and bean fields, but they seemed disturbed and would not let us get anywhere near them, flying away screeching loudly. As we got back to the village everything looked as peaceful as possible, and the guard had duly arrived. They seemed to think it part of their duty to share our room, one settling down to a comfortable smoke, the other helping to shell the beans for our evening meal. When we thought they had sufficiently studied us and our surroundings we invited them to go outside, and they soon had a cheerful fire blazing in the courtyard, where they remained all night. We got infinite amusement out of the naïve ways of our coolies and the soldiers. A heavy storm of rain, for instance, came on while we were halting at a village, and immediately one of my carriers came and sat upon the ground beside my chair in order to share the benefit of my umbrella. He had not the slightest idea, of course, that I might not wish for his close neighbourhood, for fear of participating in more than the shelter of an umbrella.

One thing seems strange as one travels day by day from one end of this great empire to the other, and that is the utter absence of any landed gentry ; never a country seat or any house larger than a farmer's, and never a garden of any kind for the cultivation of flowers except within the cities ; cottage gardens are unknown here. Pots in a courtyard show a certain love of flowers, and the poorest coolie will stop to gather a handful of camellias to decorate his load, or a flower to stick behind his ear. Rich people all love to live in big towns, where they are close to their associates.

One day the head coolie came in with our suit-cases in a state of great agitation, dragging with him a frightened-looking creature whose horse he said had pushed the luggage into the stream. To our dismay, the luggage was dripping with water, and the culprit had been hauled along to see the extent of the damage. Our usual good luck, however, had followed us ; though a new silk dressing-gown was soaked with mud and water, my sketches (next to it) had only mud traces on their backs, and nothing else was hurt. The man said he was very sorry, and evidently expected we should charge damages. He protested that he was only a poor farmer and had no means of payment. No doubt the head coolie, who is responsible for any loss and is bound to make good any breakage caused by the carelessness of the carriers, would have extorted damages from him, but as we did not, he told him to kotow; our servants sternly repeated the command, and an interested crowd of spectators watching the show added their injunctions, so that when the man grovelled in the dust and knocked his forehead on the ground, we were sorely tempted to laugh. The tragi-comic effect was irresistibly funny. It was necessary, however, to impress our men with the heinousness of the offence, lest our curios should come into greater danger. A diversion was caused by the entrance of several coolies begging me to look at their sprains, gatherings, &c., so we dismissed the poor farmer and set to work with our out-patient department. At this stage of the journey the coolies were very apt to give out a little, as the strain began to tell upon them. The weather grew warmer daily, and the crops seemed almost to grow visibly before our eyes. Fields of mustard in the plains were dazzlingly yellow and sweet-scented, and the poppies and wild roses were coming into bloom. We were struck with the beauty of various kinds of wild vines and the enormous leaves of *Senecio wilsonianus*. There are a great many varieties of these vines and of the roses, and on the eastern side of Yünnan we found particularly sweet-scented white banksia roses. Mr. Wilson, who spent a considerable time in studying the flora of China, discovered no fewer than 2000 new varieties of plants, and Messrs. Veitch of Chelsea have a most interesting collection of the plants which he brought back. The fact that he was able to bring back over 5000 specimens seems almost incredible to any one who knows the difficulties of transport. But perhaps the most striking of all the flowers that we met growing profusely in this region was the *Jasminum primulinum*, a large, brilliant jasmine of which there were the most magnificent hedges. If only we could have stayed a little longer we should have been able to see far more of the shrubs in blossom, as everywhere we noticed they were full of promise.

The architecture is more ornate in this district than in the centre of China, many of the houses in the villages being elaborately decorated, and having beautiful wooden carved screens and balustrades in front of them. Some of the shops had most knowing little beasts carved at the end of the counter, and the signboards, which were formed into Chinese lanterns, were extremely picturesque. At the entrance of one of the villages there was the most grotesque design on the large screen which is frequently to be seen facing the entrance gate of villages. This particular one had a gigantic creature (a cross between a cat and a toad) hanging on to a fleeing mouse, whose hind leg

1. VILLAGE SCREEN WALL

2. CARRYING-CHAIR

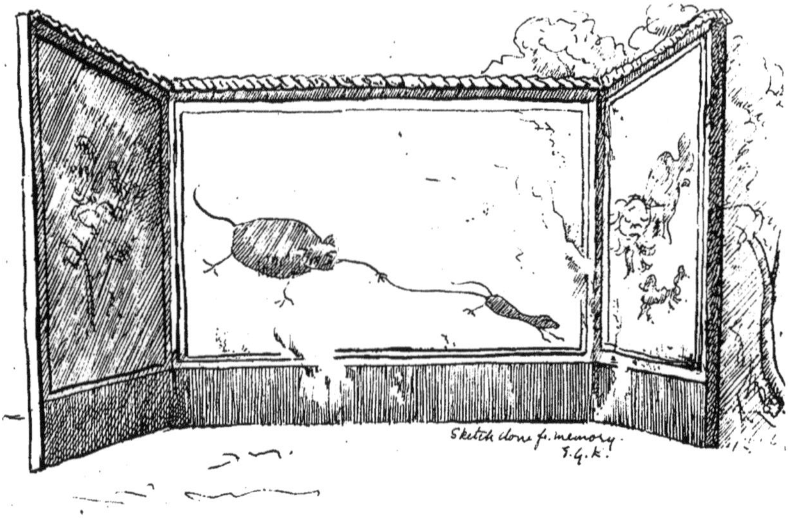

VILLAGE SCREEN WALL

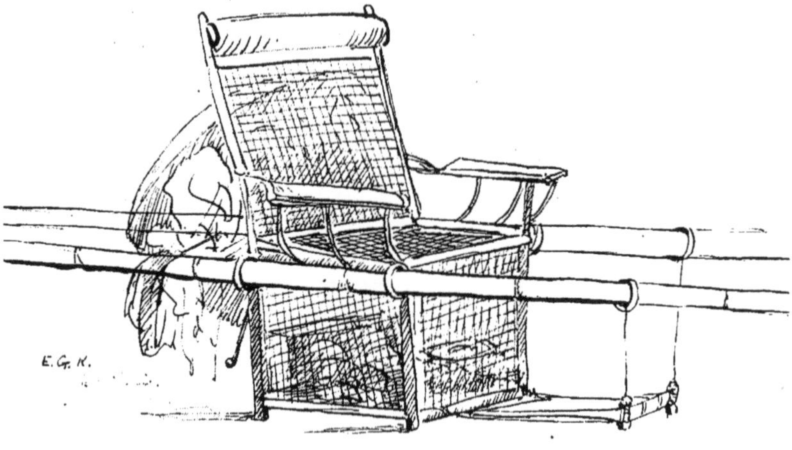

had been stretched out to an abnormal length in its endeavour to escape. Every village of any size has such a screen (called in Chinese, " shelter "), standing about fifteen feet high and twenty-five feet in length. Some of the designs on them are really artistic, but as a rule their best quality is the spirited action of the various beasts which are represented, of which the one I have sketched (from memory) is a good example. The chair below it shows what we travelled in for some 1200 miles ; the most comfortable way of seeing the country that can be imagined. Under the seat we carried all our small impedimenta, while the coolies made use of the back for theirs.

CHAPTER XXI

Tali Fu

THE first glimpse of the Tali lake with snow-capped mountains running along its western bank is very beautiful. It is a typical Chinese landscape, namely, a "mountain and water picture"; but at this time of year (the beginning of March) the winds are so high that the distant range of snow mountains to the north is invisible, and during the five days that we spent in the neighbourhood we did not once catch a glimpse of them. At the south of the lake is a large and important village, Siakwan, much more important in some respects than the prefectural town of Tali Fu itself, as it lies on the high-road from Yünnan Fu to Teng Yueh. All the trade caravans pass directly through Siakwan without branching off to Tali. At the markets, which are frequently held, there may be seen various aboriginal tribes such as the Miaos, the Lolos, the Ming Chiaos, and the Shans. The place is noted for being one of the windiest spots to be found anywhere, and we found it unpleasant both coming and going to Tali. At Tali the wind was most riotous at nights, and came in great gusts, dismantling the walls of our rooms and

TALI FU

E.G.K.

covering my bed with a little shower of photographs and texts, and nearly blowing us out of bed. The lake is always dangerous on account of these winds, and when we visited the shore, about an hour's walk from the city, there were only a few little fishing-boats to be seen close inland. The villages along it are mainly inhabited by Ming Chiaos, who speak a language of their own. It is but few comparatively of these villagers who can speak or even understand Chinese, and those who learn it do so for the sake of trading in the city. The women and girls wear their hair dressed rather differently from the Chinese, and have a different type of face. Also, they do not bind their feet, nor wear such elegant shoes. They seemed quite friendly, but were rather too inquisitive, which prevented our enjoying our picnic as much as we should have done.

I made a sketch of a little bridge with a picturesque archway in the shape of a tower leading on to it, behind which may be seen the mountains towering up to a great height. These mountains are very little known, and a European who went up to visit a temple some hours distant got lost, and was three days before he was able to find his way back ; when he returned he was quite exhausted for lack of food, and his clothes were almost torn to pieces by the bushes through which he had been obliged to force his way. There are very few inhabitants amongst these mountains, and they are of a fierce and uncertain character.

The Tali Fu women were the most pleasant and

responsive we met in the province, and some looked decidedly intelligent. They did beautiful embroidery of various kinds, and we were glad of the opportunity to order straw hats from them with which to protect ourselves from the sun. We were *not* glad, however, to see them being brought home on the heads of the woman and child; though this seems to be considered quite the correct thing in China. There was no alternative between having these particular hats or going without any, which was too risky. We are quite convinced that the wearing of a "bandeau" inside the hat must have originated in China, where the use of it is universal from the lowest to the highest. The poorest coolie has a basket bandeau in the huge, pancake-like straw hat which shelters him equally from sun or rain. The size of these hats is two feet in diameter, and the bandeaux raise them so high above the head that the effect is extremely comic, and they have to be held on by an elaborate system of strings at the sides and back, sometimes ornamented by the gayest of tassels, and with bright-green strings tied under the chin. The favourite colour of a bandeau is magenta, and the material of which it is made is satin. The portrait of myself at the beginning of this volume shows our complete travelling costume, together with the Buddhist pilgrim stick and the horn spectacles which were formerly a distinctive mark of the "scholar." On returning home we found the hats were hardly an exaggeration of the size worn in London. Liu had procured himself a different variety of straw hat (see page 211) and a bright-green waterproof cover for it.

Few foreign ladies visit Tali Fu, so our arrival created a mild excitement in the place. An official lady (the highest but one in the city) took the opportunity of paying a call on the missionary nurse who was our hostess. She had assisted at the operation performed by the doctor on the lady's daughter, who was suffering from a disfigurement of the face The lady called at the moment lunch had been served, so of course it had to be indefinitely postponed (the Chinese calls not unfrequently last for several hours). She was gorgeously attired in a heliotrope skirt embroidered with magenta and green, which had come from Chengtu, and a fur-lined plum-coloured coat. She wore gold pins galore in her hair, and a large amber bead ; gold tooth-picks and ear-picks hung from a button, and she used these with French *aplomb*. Our clothes were examined with much minuteness ; she even pinched my toe to see if it could really extend to the full length of my shoe, so I took it off to satisfy her on the subject. Perhaps it was this that encouraged her to begin to undress my friend down the back in order to see how her clothes were put on ; but the unfastening of the blouse and camisole still left it a mystery how the skirt could be made to encompass so small a waist —a problem which I fear will never be solved, for Chinese skirts are completely open down one side and are merely folded round the person. On the opposite side they also are open up to the waistband, though this does not show, owing to the upper part of the dress hanging over it. We spent some time drinking tea, and the lady talked impartially with her hostess and her hostess's servants, her own remaining in the room all the time and also drinking tea. Our ages had to be discussed, and as it appeared that mine almost coincided with her own, I learnt the interesting fact that I was born in the cycle of the dog. Owing to my fair hair I have always been considered by the Chinese to be well over eighty years of age, both now and on my previous visit. This is an extremely useful illusion, as it renders me worthy of great reverence, and made it much more proper for me to be travelling about and sitting by the high-road sketching.

The call still dragged on, and we next discussed the price of our clothes and the places we had visited, why we were unmarried, and many other topics of equal interest. After about an hour of this conversation the caller expressed a wish to see the bedrooms, and having to pass through the dining-room in order to get there, she perceived with surprise that the table was laid for a meal. The white table-cloth was a new object to her, and one of deep interest. She begged to be allowed to watch us eat, so of course she was invited to join the belated meal. While this was being brought in she went upstairs, and having inspected everything carefully, she tried the bed (poor hostess !), and asked for some "flea medicine," *alias* Keating.

We sat down to lunch, and the lady sent her servant

to bring from her sedan-chair a beautifully coloured silk serviette, which she fastened to a button at the neck of her coat with a gold clasp. She got on very well with a fork instead of chopsticks, but found the combined use of knife and fork as difficult as we did that of chopsticks. According to Chinese etiquette, all the company use their own implements to help themselves, and the dish was conveniently near to the lady! When she had no further use for the chicken bones she handed them over her shoulder to the maid, to be thrown into the courtyard; the more natural course, which would have been adopted had she been at home, would have been to put them under the table. Carpets are not in use even in the houses of the wealthy, except on special occasions such as the New Year, so that the floors are treated in the same way as the ground out of doors! Any "plat" which was not to the lady's liking was also handed to the maid to eat, and it struck us as quite a new use for servants. When the table boy was not otherwise employed, she questioned him minutely as to household arrangements, the buying of food, &c., as if his mistress were not present, and the information she received seemed to interest her vastly. She continually pressed us to eat, and did full justice to the meal herself, ladling the gravy out of the dish at intervals with her own spoon, despite the fact that she was on her way to a feast. I presented her with a piece of English ribbon and explained its use, which happily coincided with what she had already heard of English dress ; but I was disappointed that she did not follow the Chinese custom of presenting me with something in return. My curiosity to see what her gift would be was justly punished. Finally she left, seemingly well pleased with her visit, which would not have been considered at all a long one in "the middle kingdom," although we had found it somewhat exhausting.

CHAPTER XXII

Tali Fu to Teng Yueh

WE left Tali Fu on a stormy-looking morning, accompanied by the usual windy gusts, and after about a couple of miles we reached the famous temple of the goddess of mercy, the Buddhist Kwan-yin. Our coolies went in to offer incense and to invoke the goddess, as they did on their arrival at Tali Fu; for she is a great favourite with the coolie class. There is a beautiful little shrine perched on a big rock in a sort of small tank, which the goddess (under the guise of an old woman) is supposed to have brought here. In the courtyard beyond is a Buddhist temple, and in one of the side courts a temple to a famous general, containing a statue of him much more life-like than any we have yet seen. The head coolie took this opportunity of consulting the goddess as to his mother's welfare—he has not seen her for over ten years—but the answer was both unsatisfactory and vague! Our head coolie is a quaint individual, but decidedly attractive. When we gave him a tael for a pork-feast for the men he kept back part of it, and they were extremely angry. In order to appease them, he not only had to pay up, but also to give them a pork-feast on his own account. He wears a most beautiful jade bangle, and is always immaculately clean to look at, however dust-stained the rest of us may be. Some Chinamen have that delightful quality of always looking clean and keeping tidy.

When we were ready to start again the rain came down in torrents, so the men put on their hats and every one demurred to going on. There was no time to waste, however, so we insisted on setting out, and after a time the rain stopped and the wind soon dried our wet clothes. Turning down the valley after passing through Siakwan, we entered the defile through a heavy gateway, which is part of the fortifications, through which the wind tore like a hurricane, snatching off the black scarf I had wound round my hair in Chinese fashion, for it was impossible to keep on our gigantic hats. We made our way through an impressive gorge, following the river till we came to our halting-place at night. We had learnt at Tali that the official rest-houses are open to travellers when not occupied by officials, so we sent on to engage rooms in one, and certainly gained both in quality and quantity, as we occupied a sort of large barn with pillars in it, which looked as if it had formerly been used as a stable. The next night we were not so lucky, and had the most riotous party of rats in the loft above us that I have ever encountered. Their revels brought down no inconsiderable portion of the ceiling on our heads, and finally the rats themselves

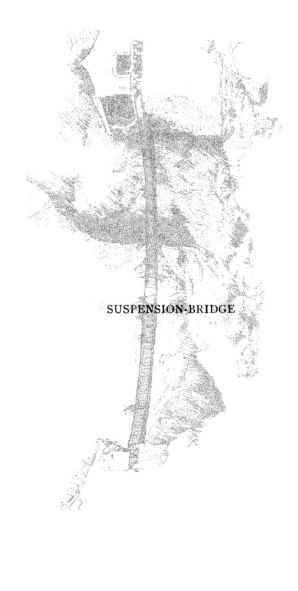

SUSPENSION-BRIDGE

came down in a sort of stampede upon us, showing no respect whatever for the British face or form. The early dawn was further made hideous by a chorus of geese, pigs, fowls, and mules, a horrid discord from which we hurried away into the lovely dew-drenched country. Crossing a suspension-bridge, we began a long, steep climb through the pine woods, and the miseries undergone were soon forgotten in the ever fresh beauties of the day. The long range of snow-capped mountains lay behind us, and for three hours we mounted higher and higher, coming to large trees of brilliant crimson rhododendrons, and various kinds of roses climbing high up amongst them.

As we sat in the shade near our coolies, taking a little rest, a stranger coolie came and sat down in his hat beside us, to the great indignation of one of our men, who promptly administered a kick in the rear. He returned the kick as soon as our man turned his back, but otherwise quite acquiesced in his dislodgment. A much dirtier man of our own then came and occupied the seat, perhaps in order to prevent any other intruder from doing so. The journey from Tali to Bhamo was one, if possible, of more beauty than any former day's travel of this beautiful tour. The hedges were ablaze with blossom, and the *Pyrus japonica* was wonderful. The size and colour of the blossom astonished us, and also the size of the plant, which is more like a tree than a shrub. The air was sweet with jasmine and orange blossom and other shrubs of which we did not know the names.

The ascents and descents grew longer and more precipitous. We saw a new variety of bridge of great interest, entirely composed of creeper. The bridge was like a hammock, but fully a hundred feet long, and very loosely woven together ; the only part of it not made of creeper was a narrow plank along the centre for walking on, and the upright poles at each end. There was a creeper hand-rail, but it would have been of very little use to hold on to it, as it was only attached at the ends.

The seventh day after leaving Tali Fu, we crossed the Mekong, a most picturesque river sunk in a narrow gorge and spanned by a fine suspension-bridge. As I sat and sketched it in the early morning the air was fragrant with wild orange blossom and jessamine, and handsome plants of orange-coloured abutilon reared themselves by the roadside. My sketching of the suspension-bridges might naturally strike the eye of the engineer as incorrect, owing to the slightness of the curve ; but the fact is that they are tightened up after construction with very great labour, by means of windlasses, till they are (comparatively speaking) horizontal. On the board above the entrance of the bridge was inscribed, "Built by the god."

The mountains are part of the great Himalayan range, and the spurs run almost directly from north to south, so that our road from east to west was always up and down. On reaching our halting-place for the night we found all the inns occupied, except one where there was a room but no beds. After much

BRIDGE MADE OF CREEPERS

EGK.

altercation, they agreed at one of the inns to turn out some of the coolies and to give us their room ; but on inspection the look of it was so unalluring that I went to see what the bedless room was like, and found a large barn over a stable, which contained nothing but a family altar and some fodder. This seemed infinitely preferable to us, especially as it had two large windows looking on to the mountains. We spread our oil-cloth on the floor and our mattresses on it, and passed a far more comfortable night than many that we had had, being undisturbed by cats or rats. Only a night or two before, a cat had raided our larder, which we thought we had made quite secure, overturning the pan, getting the lid off, and departing with our tender young chicken, of which one leg only was left in the pan. We always had to be very careful in packing up all food before going to bed, but that mattered little, as we took none in the morning before starting. Indeed, we found we required much less food on this journey than elsewhere, and two light meals a day were amply sufficient for our needs. At midday we always lunched al fresco, being set down outside the village where the men were to get their meal.

The next day after the theft we were unable to get a chicken of any sort, and the following day we had to put up with a prehistoric beast. In fact, our hands became horny from wrestling with tough fowls. Sometimes unexpected dainties turned up, and certainly we had a novel surprise on arriving at the town of Yung Chang Fu. While sitting at supper, a visiting-card was brought in from the magistrate, with a tray containing two fine ducks, two tins of sardines, and a bottle of House of Commons whisky; two lively fowls also were deposited on the floor. We sent our thanks to the magistrate for his kindness, and accepted the fowls, but returned the remainder of his gift according to custom. Our servant had vainly been trying to get a chicken for us, so the gift was most opportune, and we should have liked to thank the polite magistrate in person.

After dinner we sent for the head coolie, as this was one of the places where we paid the wages, and were amused to see him secrete thirty-six ounces of silver up his sleeve as if it were nothing. The total cost of hire for eighteen coolies from Yünnan to Bhamo, a journey which occupied thirty-three travelling days, was a little under £34.

For the first and last time in the whole of our six months' journey, we met a European on the road, and he kindly gave us permission not only to stay at his house at Teng Yueh, but gave us the keys of his store-room; having heard previously of our coming, he had given instructions to the caretaker to be on the look-out for us. In any case, we should not have been likely to miss him on the high-road, except at a spot where they have made a new road to shorten the distance, and where Liu took the opposite road from the one we did when he went ahead to get rooms.

Three days after we had crossed the Mekong, we had a stiffer climb down to the Salween, which is

2300 feet above sea-level. It has a shocking reputation for malaria, but at this season there was nothing to fear. However, I offered a dose of quinine to whoever wished to have it, and every one eagerly applied. The only member of the party who was unable to take quinine tried what is frequently found to be a good alternative, cinnamon. The Salween has a two-span bridge, connected in the centre by a fine block of masonry. The village close by seems to be inhabited by Shans, and the coolies took a long rest before beginning the toilsome ascent. We climbed up for about two hours, and were thankful for a night's rest before climbing the remaining three. We had sent one of our escort ahead in good time to secure the only inn, which was of primitive construction, and of which, as not infrequently happens, the partitions were so flimsy as to allow of a fairly good view from one room into another.

The scenery next day was particularly fine, and from this point the vegetation became semi-tropical. The monkeys barked and chattered, but kept out of sight, and we spent a long day in climbing down from the eight-thousand-foot elevation to which we had climbed so laboriously on the previous evening. The following day we reached Teng Yueh in a tearing wind. In fact, we have found the wind the most fatiguing element in our travels.

Teng Yueh (or Momein, as it was formerly called) boasts an English consulate, and we were kindly entertained there by the Consul's arrangement, although he himself was absent. His delightful Chinese major-domo received us with his best English welcome, and delighted us by at once asking "Missee want hot bath?" "Other Missee want hot bath?" and promptly went to get them ready. He proved to be the most attentive of servants, and told us we were to ask for whatever we wanted. Naturally, the first requisite seemed a washerwoman, and he promised to send "catchee female," and the next morning he introduced an elegant native laden with jewelry. To a further request that he would procure a small piece of mutton for us to take on our journey, he said, "No can catchee mutton, but goat very good."

The neighbourhood of Teng Yueh is picturesque, surrounded by mountains, and the town itself is more open and clean than most. The people have pleasant manners and are friendly to the foreigner. There is a new Custom House and post-office, and houses for the European staff, which are not yet all completed. These stand out conspicuously, surrounded by their walls, and we saw them many miles away as we descended from the mountains. We felt that this was our last chance of getting Chinese things, so we spent the afternoon shopping, but were not altogether successful. The jade for which the place is celebrated we found more expensive than we had expected, and there did not seem much choice. The threatening look of the sky made us procure waterproof hat-covers at one penny apiece, and they proved quite efficacious in dispersing the clouds. There were

pine-apples, bananas, tomatoes, and various vegetables in the market; and we also succeeded in buying postage-stamps, of which we had found the post-office of Tali Fu practically empty. We had some difficulty, in fact, in getting them at most of the post-offices in the province of Yünnan.

And now we started on our last Chinese journey, after one day's rest, feeling each day more regretful at the thought that it would so soon be ended. The days grew hotter and the wind stronger, and the road not nearly so beautiful, and the inns decidedly worse, yet still we looked back with wistful eyes to the "Flowery Land" (so justly named) we had passed through. The country seemed mainly inhabited by Shans, a fine, well-built race, very clean-looking, and the women picturesquely dressed. Most of them were entirely dressed in black, with large silver ornaments, and they looked very attractive with jaunty bunches of jasmine stuck in their tall black turbans. Their villages looked quite different from the Chinese villages. The inns look miserable, but are less abject than they appear; and when, to my surprise, in the dim light I saw through the airy bamboo screen (which formed the wall) a portly pig arise from my side, I thought how often one had passed much less comfortable nights in pleasanter surroundings! I think the pig must have taken up her residence there when I was asleep.

From Teng Yueh to Bhamo the route lies all the way along the river-side of the Taping, and the first part of it is most tiresome, as it is constantly in the shingly bed of the river itself, where the heat of the sun is reflected from the stones. Our coolies' clothing grew daily less, and even the chilly creature who wore an eighteenpenny skin coat discarded it. In fact, the coolies began to look like the conventional pictures of John the Baptist with one bare arm exposed to view. One of our attentive boys always presented us with our hats when he thought it time to put them on in the morning on account of the heat. We tied them very securely to our chairs ever since one of the coolies thought fit to carry my friend's hat on his own head.

There was an amusing theatrical performance of an elementary kind held close to our inn in a small village. It was a sort of votive offering as a thanksgiving for the recovery of a sick person. The stage was in the middle of the road. It consisted in a table and a small bench in front of it, on which stood the principal figure, representing the Emperor. He recited a good deal under the large flowing beard which covered his mouth, and which he occasionally pretended to pull. As it was attached with string round his ear, a slight tweak would have detached it. Before him stood three gaudily dressed figures, who made a few dance steps at intervals, and turned round; they also recited now and then. Their main occupation, however, seemed to be fanning themselves and expectorating. When they got tired they withdrew behind the table for tea, and the Emperor twitched off his beard and imperial clothes in the twinkling of an eye, with an air of infinite relief. The clothes were thrown into a large basket which seemed to contain all the stage properties. The spectators were really the most interesting part of the show, as several of the women had evidently got on their best clothes, and fine silver ornaments all over their high turbans, and massive necklaces and bangles. We were beginning at last to get away from the prevalent plague of goitre, and it was a relief to see clean, healthy people again.

CHAPTER XXIII

From China into Burma

GRADUALLY the scenery changed as we approached British territory, and then, quite suddenly, the vegetation became tropical within a day's march of the frontier. The trees are much more lofty, and rise as straight as darts up into the blue. Often they are strangled by the huge creepers which wind round and round them, and seem to draw their life-blood from the trees which they kill, becoming almost as large in the trunk, and with great bloated leaves concealing their victims. Long feelers hang down from the tree-tops, and orchids and ferns grow profusely, high up among the branches. Everything possesses a brilliancy and size and vitality which has in it something fearful; indeed, it is as if it were an evil power brooding over everything and crushing weaker things in a relentless grasp. The spider-webs are like gauze handkerchiefs spread over the banks, in the centre of which are gaping doorways, where you see the monster spider sprawling with an insolent, will-you-walk-into-my-parlour air. The monkeys chatter and jabber unseen; some of them—the "gibbons"—are of a large size. Parrots scream, and modest-plumaged familiar birds are replaced by brilliant ones with shrill, unsympathetic voices. We met, too, various tribes-people, such as Shans and Kachins.

Our spirits fell somewhat, too, at the thought of leaving China, of parting from our pleasant company, and ending the most delightful tour we had ever had. The last night we spent at a "head man's" house, but his Excellency was away from home. We had a pleasant upstairs room overlooking a large courtyard filled with pack-animals, whose driver slept with them in the open, according to custom, despite a terrific thunderstorm in the middle of the night. There was no door to our room, but we hung up a curtain, and a soldier slept just outside. Mr. Ku and Liu slept one on each side of the family altar downstairs. We started next morning at the usual hour, and after some miles our military escort took leave of us, at the edge of the stream which divides the two greatest empires in the world. A rude trunk acted as bridge, and we saw Liu timorously hesitating on the edge, till one of the coolies took pity on him and came and handed him across. As this was the first time that our men had been on British soil (with the exception of two of them), we felt we ought to do something to celebrate the event, and I was very anxious that they should look their best when we came to the British outpost. It was in vain, however, that I had offered to have them all shaved and coiffed, as I found it would practically take a day to get it done ; and also there was a difficulty in even procuring a barber in any of the adjoining villages. It is astounding the difference the shaving makes in their appearance, as the larger part of the head is kept shaved. We had to give up the hope of making a brave show, but this did not signify so much when we found that there was no British outpost. In fact, the only thing that marked the difference of territory was that now we came on to a splendid road and found excellent bridges. We promised the men "tooth-worship" (namely, pork-feast) that evening, but there was nothing very attractive to be obtained when we got to the extremely imperfect inn where we halted for the night. It was a bamboo erection, rather like cellular clothing in its porousness, and, as usual, our room lay in the centre. The place was conspicuously large, airy, and clean, but it required all our luggage and the curtains to make any sort of screen. After supper we set out all our empty tins and bottles, as there is nothing which coolies esteem more. They had been begging us all the time to give them our biscuit-tins, which were the greatest prizes, though jam- and butter-tins were useful for cooking purposes. The biscuit-tins had been promised to those who were thought most deserving. When they put them in our chairs for us, they would tap them and give us a wink, as much as to say, "This is going to be mine some day," or shake them to see if they were nearly empty. By this time we had got a thoroughly large selection, and had an amusing time in distributing them. The men also petitioned for quinine to take with them for recrossing the Salween; each man received two doses, to his great satisfaction.

The last morning dawned; for the last time we heard the familiar awakening cry, "Arise, wash your faces, eat your rice," and we reluctantly made our way along the beautiful road through the forest, a road such as the coolies had never seen before. We had ordered a *gharri* (=carriage) to meet us ten miles from the town, as it was too long for a one day's stage, now that the hot weather had set in; so we arranged for the men and coolies to follow us to Bhamo the next day with our chairs and luggage. We halted at the Dak Bungalow, where we were met by one of our friends from Bhamo, and after tea we transferred our requisites to the *gharri* and set out for Bhamo. As we rattled along in the noisy and uncomfortable vehicle we longed for our comfortable chairs, but were soon pulled up short by the harness giving way. A piece of cloth proved ineffectual to hold it together for more than about half a mile. I then provided a piece of string which proved more efficacious, but only a few minutes later there was a hopeless crash as the axle split in two between the front wheels. We had to sit down ignominiously by the roadside for at least an hour, while the man rode off on the horse to get another carriage. Oh, to be back in China, where we found things so slow and steady!

Next morning our men arrived with the luggage,

and after settling accounts with them and presenting them with the two sedan-chairs and our carrying-poles, we regretfully bade them good-bye. I think the desire was exceedingly strong on both sides that we should meet again and have just such another journey. With many journeys it requires the mellowing distance of time to forget the disagreeables, but we had but one thought in looking back, and that was one of entire satisfaction.

CHAPTER XXIV

The Present Situation in China

SINCE the preceding chapters were written great changes have taken place in the Chinese Empire, and a new reign has begun. The sudden, simultaneous death of the Emperor and the Dowager Empress at first caused a feeling of general consternation; but it soon became evident that the reins of government had passed into strong and capable hands. The Regent has already shown that he intends to pursue the policy of his predecessor, both with regard to external and internal matters, and reform is the order of the day.

In the concluding pages of this volume I venture to give a brief summary of the special points under consideration at the present time, which foreshadow the changes to be expected in the near future. It is impossible for any one, no matter how intimately acquainted with Chinese affairs, to foretell what will be the outcome of the great constitutional change which is contemplated; but it is of importance that the European public should understand the conditions under which it takes place. It would be presumption on my part to do anything more than call attention to the problems and the difficulties which beset the path of the reformer.

At the present time the government of China is an absolute monarchy, and as the new Emperor is but four years old, the supreme power is vested in a Regent, his father, Prince Chun: he was really appointed by the late Dowager Empress, though nominally by the Emperor. The Regent is assisted by a Grand Council, composed of five leading State officials, and contains some of the ablest statesmen in the Empire. There are, moreover, several boards for the control and management of various State departments, such as the Wai wupu, the Board for Foreign Affairs (formerly called the Tsung Li Yamen); the Lung-kung-shangpu, the Board of Agriculture, Industry, and Commerce; the Tuchihpu, the Board of Finance; the Boards of Education, of Justice, of War, of Naval Affairs, &c.; but all these boards are under the absolute control of the Regent. He has the supreme authority, and can depose, banish, or execute at will, and without any form of trial, any official of whatsoever rank, as was seen in the recent case of H.E. Yuan Shih Kai, one of the ablest Chinese statesmen and one of the leading figures in educational reform. The Regent appoints all officials on these several boards, all viceroys and governors of provinces, and all envoys to foreign countries. Since the troubles of 1900 there has been a growing desire for constitutional reform, and a few years ago H.E. Tuan Fang, Viceroy of the Liangkiang, was despatched on a mission of investigation to several large European countries, to America, and to Japan. I cannot do better than quote his own words as to the result of his mission. They form part of a preface written by him (as an introduction) to Green's "Short History of the English People," which has recently been translated into Chinese. "In the various civilised countries my object was to select and compare their constitutions. Arriving in London, I saw the excellent order of the constitution in ruler and people. In Japan's reformation she got much from England; much more will our country by-and-by take England for her model. . . . Excellent is the word of Dr. Macklin [the translator], 'If you desire to establish a constitution you must follow England. To follow England you must read English history.'"

The determination has been arrived at to have a representative assembly; other envoys have been sent to Europe to obtain fuller information about constitutional methods, and measures are being taken to prepare the Chinese people for the momentous change. The development of local government is an important step in this direction, and the Regent has strongly commended the successful work done in the Liang-kiang provinces, urging others to follow the good example of H.E. Tuan Fang. The elective body will be a very limited one: it will consist of (i) all holders of literary degrees (students only holding degrees granted by Christian colleges are debarred from voting); (ii) all holders of property to the amount of 5000 taels (about £750). Those eligible for the vote are further restricted by the prohibition against opium-smokers, Buddhist monks, &c. The date is not yet fixed for the summoning of the first assembly, but it is proposed that it should take place in the fourth year of the present reign.

The salient characteristic of the present Government is the divorce of the executive from the legislative faculty. Edicts are issued incessantly, but very little is done to give practical effect to the majority of them. Official corruption is almost universal, and the difficulties of combating it are so great that many good men are deterred from entering official life because they feel the impossibility of putting a stop to bribery in their own Yamens. Up to the present time bribery has been legitimatised and nothing done to check it, except in flagrant cases; now there is to be a serious attempt made to put it down, and the fact is recognised that it is a public wrong, as may be seen from the edict quoted on page 129.

While the general public in China does not show much interest in the question of representative government, nor indeed understand anything about it, there is a growing interest taken in the question of social reforms. One of the most pressing ones is that of prison reform. The extra-territoriality agreement is a source of constant irritation to the Chinese, although they are forced to admit the necessity for it, so long as the administration, the prisons, and the laws are in such an unsatisfactory condition. Commissioners have been appointed to thoroughly investigate the whole question and to study European prison methods, while newspaper intelligence informs us that a gallows has been imported from Great Britain! New prisons are being erected in many places, but that is the least important change which humanity demands.

Of more importance than prison reform is the opium question. Since the conference at Shanghai in the early part of this year more strenuous efforts are being made to combat the evil, and real progress is reported from those parts of the Empire where officials are loyally and enthusiastically enforcing the imperial decrees. In a report of H.E. Tuan Fang it is stated that during the three years which have elapsed since the anti-opium campaign was started 60 per cent. of the smokers have given up the habit. The mowage of the poppy-planted ground and the number of opium shops have been decreased more than 50 per cent.

From the province of Yunnan, where we saw much poppy cultivation, news comes that the traveller sees practically none; from Szechwan and Shansi similar reports state that other crops have entirely replaced the poppy except in isolated districts. Opium dens are being closed, and fines and other punishments are imposed on growers and sellers of the drug. In addition to the severe penalties already in force, yet worse are to follow in case opium-smoking is not abandoned within the prescribed time limit. From the current year—according to a recent edict—to the fifth year of Hsuan Tung the maximum penalty for officials smoking opium is *strangulation*; in the sixth year this penalty is to be extended to the gentry, and in the seventh to the common people. There is no doubt but that China is in real earnest in her determination to root out what she considers the worst evil in her national life, and it will be a disgrace to the British Empire if we let selfish considerations prevent our loyal co-operation with her. What is to be said of such double-dealing as is shown in the fact that the British Government has agreed to reduce the import of opium from India, and to let it entirely cease by 1917, provided the Chinese Government shows her sincerity in putting down the traffic, while at the same time the very efforts made by the Chinese officials are checkmated by the protests of his Majesty's Government? This has actually stopped the splendid work of H.E. Tuan Fang in the Kiangsu province during the last two years. "His action was suspended on the protest of his Majesty's Government that it came in conflict with treaty provisions. The whole scheme is now in abeyance," &c.[1]

Other difficulties which China has to face in dealing with the opium question are set forth in an imperial decree of March 15, 1909:—

"Opium suppression is a necessary measure to the

[1] Extract from Sir John Jordan's correspondence with the Foreign Office—Paper *China*, No. 1, 1908, page 36. For full details of this matter, see Arnold-Forster's "International Commission for the Investigation of the Opium Trade" (Hodder & Stoughton).

strengthening of our Empire, as well as the mainspring of the development and instruction of the people, involving, as it does, questions of hygiene, of enriching the people, of developing terrestrial profits, and of arresting a drain on the national wealth. All eyes are turned to this subject, and much universal sympathy and assistance have been exhibited.

"On the question, three steps are closely interrelated and dependent, and these are: prohibition of smoking and of plantation, and devising of means to raise revenue to fill the deficit caused in the opium duties. Should any one of these be inefficiently carried out, the other two will in consequence be hampered, and success would be looked for in vain.

"In recent years, though officials addicted to the smoking habit have been examined and denounced on repeated occasions by the Anti-Opium Commissioners and Viceroys and Governors of the provinces, there still exists a number of them who trifle with the interdict and veneer their faults in that respect.

"With regard to the prohibition of the poppy plantation in the provinces, it was first decided to decrease the plantation gradually in ten years. Later, the authorities of Yunnan, Szechwan, Shansi, Chili, Heilungkiang, and other provinces asked permission to forbid plantation entirely in one year. This, no doubt, shows great energy of purpose; but whether their intention is thoroughly carried out in all their provinces, and whether the local officials succeed in inducing the people to plant other profitable products on their soil to yield them a living so that they gladly submit to the suppression, remains to be seen.

"The duties and likin on this drug are required for the bulk of the army estimates. Recently the Ministry of Finance memorialised us and obtained permission to increase the price of salt to make up for these duties and likin. This plan, however, only aggregates four or five million taels, and there still remains a large deficit.

"We are eagerly bent on introducing a better government, and between our agitation at the long weakness of our people, in whom it is difficult to infuse energy, and the fear that the expectations of the friendly Powers may not be easily satisfied, we are filled with constant and pressing anxiety. We hereby reiterate the prohibition against smoking. The Anti-Opium Commissioners and the high officials in the capital and provinces are held responsible to forbid, faithfully and with energy, all officials, civil or military, to smoke. Those in command of troops or in charge of educational institutions are made responsible for suppression of smoking among soldiers and students. As to merchants and the people, the responsibility must rest with the Ministry of the Interior, the Viceroys, Governors, Military Governors, and the Governor of the Imperial Prefecture of Shuntienfu. They will try to obtain the best prescriptions, establish anti-opium institutes, and distribute free medicines when necessary. They should encourage their sense of honour, and adopt the plans and practices of foreign countries, so that the people's vices may be gradually lessened and finally eradicated.

"As to the prohibition of plantation, Viceroys or Governors, the Governor of the Imperial Prefecture of Shuntienfu, and Military Governors are commanded to direct their subordinates to carry out the suppression with care and thoroughness. They should also cause other grains to be planted in place of the pernicious drug, and they will be rewarded according to the degree of success they attain. The Ministry of the Interior will supervise these measures being put in operation.

"In regard to devising means to fill the deficit of duties and likin, the Ministry of Finance is desired carefully to consider the question. It is, undoubtedly, an important point to be dealt with, but it may be disposed of by weighing advantages and drawbacks and considering all possible resources. Viceroys and Governors who may have valuable suggestions on the question are ordered to memorialise the Throne for their adoption, so that those carrying out the suppression need not be hampered by financial considerations. Though the Government is in straitened circumstances, it will neither seek to satisfy its hunger nor quench its thirst at the expense of this harmful poison, so that it may rid its people of this great bane.

"Dividing, in this way, the responsibilities and actions, no evasion of burden will be permitted, and all concerned are commanded to put forth their best energies to aid us in securing prosperous rule by taking natural advantages to ameliorate the conditions of life among our people. After receipt of this Edict each office in the capital or provinces is commanded to make a careful report of its plan of operation in this affair."

[The above edict is sealed by the Prince Regent, and is signed by the Grand Councillors Prince Ching, Shih Hsü, Chang Chih-tung, and Lu Ch'uan-lin.]

This decree leads us to another problem the solution of which will task the ablest of her statesmen, namely, the financial problem. It may well be that she would be wiser to seek foreign expert knowledge to grapple with it, rather than to tide over present difficulties by having recourse to foreign loans.

There seems no reasonable doubt that China possesses untold mineral wealth, and that railway enterprise ought also to become a valuable source of income. Foreign nations have realised it only too well, and railway and mining concessions have been granted, which China is now trying to win back into her own hands. She has not been altogether faithful to her agreements, and the foreign Powers remind one of a pack of snarling hounds quarrelling over the booty. It is certain that China cannot dispense at the present time with foreign assistance, but she would probably find it more profitable in the long run to obtain the best expert knowledge, and to pay for it, rather than to try and make bargains and to obtain quick returns. At the present time the mineral wealth of the country can only be successfully developed under the direction of trained Europeans, but the Chinese—not unnaturally, one must admit—are suspicious of foreign aid. The mining concessions already granted to foreign nations are a constant source of friction, and entail perpetual controversy. Misunderstandings inevitably arise.

Perhaps the most important of all the changes taking place in China to-day is in its system of education. It has been somewhat unfairly said that the only things she cared for in her old educational scheme were Scholarship and Style. Had there not been some more vital quality in it, it could hardly have held on so securely for many hundred years. That vital element may have been the love of *morals* so inseparably connected with scholarship in China. Now the old system has been completely abolished, and the Chinese classics are in danger of being relegated to the background. As soon as the change was commenced by the abolition of the triennial examinations thousands of students flocked to Japan, eager to absorb the new learning which was to replace the old. This was no difficult task in one way, for the cultivation of the memory was the main object of the former education, and they learnt what was taught them with a readiness which naturally led them to suppose that they had mastered a subject when they had committed its terms to memory. The result was as unsatisfactory as might have been anticipated; for they merely brought home with them a second-hand, unassimilated collection of information without any satisfactory foundation. Japanese influence, which was paramount after the amazing success of Japan during the recent war, soon waned, and even the Japanese themselves have deplored the rashness of their policy with regard to China.[1] The returned students were by no means fitted for the position of becoming teachers of "Young China." The impossibility of obtaining competent teachers of Western science for so vast an empire as China must be obvious to every one, and the appointment of unqualified teachers has brought much confusion into the schools. The spirit of unrest and insubordination has been steadily growing, and the Government has tried to check this by enjoining a stricter worship of Confucius.

In mission schools the influence of this spirit has also been felt, although in a less degree. It is of the utmost importance that all missions should do their best to counteract this feeling and to inculcate loyalty and obedience, while endeavouring as far as possible to correlate the education with that given in the Government schools. They are seriously handicapped by the much larger salaries now offered by Government in order to get capable teachers, and the missions must be prepared to make large sacrifices if they are to continue the educational work which they have so successfully inaugurated. They have at least 1500 primary schools, in which there are not less than 30,000 scholars. In these the teaching

[1] See Count Okuma's article in "The Far East."

is usually superior to that of the Government schools, but the equipment is very inferior.

It would be out of place to describe here the various schemes which are now being put before the British public for carrying on the education of those trained in mission schools into the higher branches of knowledge implied in a college training, but it is of supreme importance that the education which is given by Europeans—whether in mission or in other schools—should be first-rate in quality. It were better, if need be, to restrict the scope of operations rather than allow any defect in the quality of the work. It has been the tendency of most missions to undertake more work than they could successfully cope with ; and while admiring the results they have achieved, often under a heavy strain, I cannot but hope that in the future a more generous support, especially in the matter of increased staff, will be given to those who are labouring for the educational regeneration of China.

An increasing number of students are going to Great Britain and America for education, but it is recognised that there are difficulties and dangers in this course. One of the most far-sighted of China's statesmen, H.E. Tuan Fang has instituted a wise scheme of preparation for such students. There is an annual examination held at Nanking for all students going abroad under Government auspices. In 1907 eighty-four candidates presented themselves, of whom seventy-two were men and twelve women.

They were examined in the following subjects: English composition, translation from English into Chinese and *vice versa*, Latin, French, German, chemistry, physics and physiology, history, geography, Chinese composition, geometry, trigonometry, algebra. The only failures were in languages.

In a recent lecture to the China Society, Mr. Cantlie stated the fact that the average size of the Chinese brain is greater than that of any other race; and certainly the students who have come over to Europe show a capacity of not only keeping up with our students in their work, but frequently of surpassing them.

The whole civilised world looked on with astonishment and admiration at the rapid evolution of the Japanese nation in recent times, and now the Chinese Empire has resolved to make a similar change. It has a much more difficult task to achieve, and one which, on account of the size of the Empire, is likely to have a far greater importance for the world at large. The Chinese are strongly animated by the spirit of patriotism; they have great qualities of heart and mind, and a set determination to carry through the necessary reforms. In the dark ages of the past they were the pioneers in art, science, and philosophy; therefore one can with hopefulness look forward to a yet nobler future, and trust that the new era which is beginning may be one of ever-increasing greatness for the Celestial Empire.

TABLE OF THE PRINCIPAL CHINESE DYNASTIES

LEGENDARY Chinese history extends from the twenty-ninth to the tenth century B.C., the first dynasty emerging from the mists being the

Chow dynasty	1122 to 249 B.C.
Han ,,	206 B.C. to 220 A.D.
Tang ,,	618 A.D. to 906 A.D.
Sung ,,	960 ,, ,, 1279 ,,
Yuan (the Mongol)	1280 ,, ,, 1367 ,,
Ming	1368 ,, ,, 1643 ,,
Ching, or Ts'ing (Manchu)	1643 to the present day.

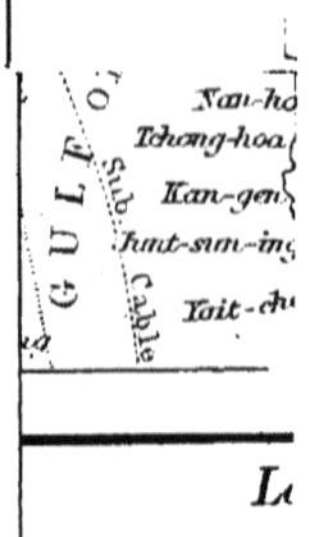
GULF O
Sub. Cable
Nan-ho
Tchong-hoa
Kan-gen
Yoit-ch
Lo

YELLOW SEA
HUNAN
HUPEH
CANTON
FORMOSA OR TAIW
Rashoo Channel

INDEX

Index

Index

Index

Printed by BALLANTYNE, HANSON & Co
Edinburgh & London

Lightning Source UK Ltd.
Milton Keynes UK
UKHW020940110219
337097UK00012B/864/P

9 781333 790387